INTERFLUG
East Germany's Airline

Sebastian Schmitz

Designed by Simon De Rudder

Second edition
Copyright © 2025 Astral Horizon Press. All rights reserved.

Astral Horizon Press

www.astralhorizon.co.uk
www.theairlineboutique.com

ISBN 978-1-9160396-3-6

Printed in the Netherlands

Danke

Many people played a role in developing the idea for this book, most notably Charles Kennedy, the publisher and editor, who liked the idea immediately when I suggested it to him years ago – and his colleagues at Astral Horizon Press, Tegan Rielly, Steve Finnigan and Bhavna Vadher. Then of course Simon de Rudder, who did the beautiful design. André Skrabania helped find many of the beautiful pictures; he is part of the team at the Il-62 museum in Stölln and produces a beautiful Interflug calendar each year (have a look: www.reprowings.com). Matthias Winkler supplied some great pictures from his collection and Andreas Spaeth was kind enough to write a fascinating guest chapter and sent in pictures from the memorable flights he took on Interflug. Thanks to Theo Handstede and Luc Bereni for sharing their memories with me (I would have loved to fly Interflug so badly and am deeply jealous). Daniel Frohriep-Ichihara often pointed me in the right direction, finding people to speak to and opening his treasure chest of a collection to me. Thanks a lot to Hannelore Mildes and Marianne Jacobs-Dahlmann as well as André Skrabania once more for sharing their flight attendant memories and lovely moments and good laughs on the telephone or in person. Many more people allowed me to use their pictures, read their stories, supplied a safety card or postcards from their collection: Tino Lehmann, Guy van Herbruggen, Alan Bushell, Gottfried Schilke, Ralf Manteufel, Dirk Peisker, Athanasios. Thank you also to Susan Roller, Lesley Turner, Charles Gowlland, Keith Phillimore, Jeremy Major.

Contents

Berlin Calling: foreword by Charles Kennedy	6
What's in a name: how Deutsche Lufthansa became Interflug	10
The Ilyushin Il-14: the first people mover	14
The Antonov An-24 and GDR domestic flying	20
A small excursion by train	26
The Baade 152: a homegrown jetliner	30
The Ilyushin Il-18: long haul turboprop	36
The Tupolev Tu-134: jet power at last	42
The Ilyushin Il-62: the flagship	52
The Tupolev Tu-154: why Interflug never flew them	62
Interflug colours as camoflage: the aircaft of TG-44 and Stasi	66
Interflug crews: a privileged bunch?	76
Crew episodes	84
Solidarity flights and charter work	94
The first German low-cost airline	102
Interflug in advertising and popular culture	106
Five in one	112
Interflug, Interhotel, Intershop	118
Interflug's darkest days	122
Airbus A310: Interflug's only widebody	128
Interflug's short-lived Dash 8	136
Interflug eyewitness reports	140
Experiencing Interflug right after the wall fell	148
The end	154
Berline: the most successful survivor (at least for a while)	162
Interflug survivors on display	168
A village with an Ilyushin	178

Berlin Calling:
foreword by Charles Kennedy

The airline business is always political. In the early and middle eras of its evolution, it was primarily a function of statehood, with national carriers flying to the great cities of the world to ferry the nation's emissaries and high value exports out, and bring new expertise and tourism dollars in, with the colours of the flag taking their place in the line up of tail fins at the various air crossroads as a projection of soft power, as symbolic as a flag fluttering in the East River breeze outside the United Nations building in New York.

And perhaps there has never been an airline as political as Interflug, the national airline of the German Democratic Republic (GDR), the dictatorland Eastern half of Germany that fell inside the Soviet sphere of influence after the war. To the world, Interflug was a tangible symbol of a start-up nation that sought legitimacy, with uneven results, throughout its entire existence. And within the GDR, air travel bestowed evidence of mobility and status, two of the rarest commodities in the country.

To be fair, the state was able to deliver air travel in some form to many – while pole-vaulting across the Inner German Border (even the regular flight to Amsterdam took a circuitous route north via Danish airspace) and visiting the West remained almost impossible, a domestic hop even on short distances was a viable alternative to the poor intercity roads in the post-war GDR, and a holiday inside the socialist bloc at a Black Sea resort such as Sochi, Bourgas or Odessa was an option for many through work associations and sports clubs. For the privileged few in the upper strata of GDR society, there was Havana.

This book, the first on Interflug in the English language, tells the fascinating story of this unusual airline, its mission, its fleet, and what it was like to fly on it, to work there, and to live in those times. While there is nothing in the GDR's human rights record of surveillance, political imprisonment, and even torture that should evoke any nostalgia, the tensions and strangeness that resulted from the contradictions and weaknesses in the state's founding dogma created a fascinating world that is rightly worthy of remembering and even enjoying.

A couple of angles on Interflug I always find fascinating. For one thing, it is the only hometown airline of any significance that Berlin has ever had. West Berlin's Tegel Airport hosted a small American-owned charter outfit called Air Berlin USA, but post-reunification when it became a German-owned major carrier, Air Berlin did more flying out of Dusseldorf. West Germany's airline hub was (and in united Germany remains) Frankfurt, so for Lufthansa, Berlin has only ever been a spoke, and even that spoke is a post-reunification development, as German airlines were barred from serving West Berlin for the entire duration of the partition of Germany, under the terms of the post-World War 2 settlement. Yes, in the entire period of 1945 to 1991, West Berlin was only permitted airline service by airlines of the Soviet Union, the United States, France and the United Kingdom (and pilots had to be citizens of those countries). So during the Cold War years, the biggest airline in West Berlin was Pan Am, which went bust the same year as the Soviet Union. Germans always insist the Berlin isn't real Germany, but a rather eccentric and wilful relative, so how apt that instead of deluxe and efficient Lufthansa or LTU, Berlin got Interflug. No sleek Boeings to New York, but plenty of cranky Ilyushins to Luanda, Karachi and Pyongyang.

Another interesting quirk of Interflug is how out of sync the hardware was with the West – for instance, Lufthansa received its first Airbus A320s in 1989, very much a product of today with a digital cockpit and fly-by-wire controls, the same year Interflug were still receiving brand-new coal-burning Ilyushin Il-62s. Like parking a Prius next to craft lifted from Jules Verne's *voyages extraordinaire*.

To continue down a path of fantasy into alternative universes, is there one where Interflug survived reunification, or East German history took a different turn? Whereas the United States foresaw a prosperous and allied West Germany as a strategic footprint in the heart of Europe as well as a bulwark against future conflict, the Soviet Union, which lost 26 million citizens in the conflagration, was not in a conciliatory mood at the cessation of hostilities in May 1945, and unbolted most of the surviving industrial infrastructure in its East German sphere of control as a form of rough reparations, and saddled the nascent GDR with debts to be paid to Moscow banks for decades.

If the GDR had instead been showered with cash and technology, how different might its trajectory have been? The main motivation for so many East Germans to escape their country was the lack of freedom or material wealth. If the system had been more accommodating or generous, the need to restrict freedom would have been greatly reduced. Could there be a different GDR out there, a successful country demonstrating the benefits of socialism, with high quality exports, including a thriving aerospace sector, perhaps even a space programme

DDR-SES, a 1986-vintage Ilyushin Il-62M, resting between long haul assignments at Berlin Schönefeld
Alan Bushell
Previous page: Interflug ticket office in Damascus in 1968
Ulrich Kohls via Bundesarchiv

Tu-134 in good company at Schönefeld Interflug Abteilung Werbung

following in the footsteps of GDR kids TV's adventurous Sandman puppet, matching the achievements in space of its ideological adversary across the Atlantic, and its comrade to the east. I always assume the space station in Andrei Tarkovsky's 1972 sci fi epic Solaris is a product of the Tupolev space design bureau, but perhaps cosmonaut Kris Kelvin's great battle of conscience takes place aboard a Baade? More plausibly, the Baade 152 jetliner could have marked the beginning of an airliner dynasty with the GDR exporting jets to airlines throughout the socialist and non-aligned world, and in later years contributing parts and expertise to Airbus.

That's a universe far from the GDR that was hobbled by the post war settlement with the Soviet Union and the lack of freedom that went with it. A revolution against the unending austerity of the system was inevitable (even if it felt immoveable for many decades, indeed right up until it ended). But did Interflug have to leave us so soon?

With different interests and different timing, there could totally have been an Interflug-Condor or Interflug-LTU tie up, or a big contract with a West Berlin tour operator, flying Germans from both East and West to the beach for a few more years aboard those 1980s-build Il-62s. A steam punk expressway between East Berlin's 90s techno scene and the clubs of Ibiza. Followed by a metamorphosis into a boutique airline for central Europe, operating a hub and spoke network out of Schönefeld and joining one of the big three airline alliances (given the overtures made between Interflug and British Airways in the final days, and Lufthansa's membership of Star Alliance, the smart money would be on oneworld – so throw in a close marketing and technical agreement with Russia's Sibir/S7, who are themselves an enthusiastic operator of Baade RJs in our alternative reality).

So that's a glimpse of a few alternate timelines we didn't get to experience (but who's to say they didn't happen just a few short dimensions from here). The Interflug we had was interesting enough by far – an all-politics-all-the-time route map making landfall at the most unlikely of places (no Berlin airport today has service to any of Interflug's long haul destinations), flown aboard smoky Soviet jetliners sporting that dashing and iconic red livery. Comrades, your flight to Berlin is ready. All aboard!

Claygate, England
June 2020

What's in a name?
How Deutsche Lufthansa became Interflug

After the end of World War Two, no civilian flying by German airlines took place. It was only in 1955, a decade after the end of the war, that Germany's airspace was cleared for civilian flights once more and German airlines would be allowed to fly passengers after this decade-long hiatus.

Before the war, Deutsche Lufthansa had been the dominant carrier for Germany. Founded in 1926, Lufthansa served quite a comprehensive network and airports like Berlin or Leipzig were important departure points. As the war progressed, civilian flying became more problematic and in April 1945, just days before Germany's capitulation, Lufthansa operated its last scheduled passenger flight. With the end of the war, the Allies placed aviation over German territory under their control and banned all civilian flights.

In 1951, the remaining assets of what was effectively the first Lufthansa were liquidated and the company's history came to a temporary end. At the same time, in the early 1950s and both in West and East Germany, preparations started for the day when civilian passengers would be allowed once more. In West Germany, a company called LUFTAG (Aktiengesellschaft für Luftverkehrsbedarf) was founded in 1953, four Lockheed L-1049G Super Constellations were ordered and management worked to get everything in place for the resumption of flights once the Allies gave the green light. Pilots and cabin attendants were trained and in September 1954, LUFTAG purchased and registered the trademark rights to the Lufthansa name and logo. In April 1955, scheduled Lufthansa flights in West Germany resumed with an initial fleet of four Convair 340s.

In East Germany, preparations for a resumption of civilian passenger flights started a bit later; the first Ilyushin Il-14 piston prop built under licence by Elbe Flugzeugwerke in Dresden was handed over at Schönefeld Airport in July 1955. Maybe because the people in charge were simply used to "Deutsche Lufthansa" being the name of the German airline from their pre-war days, they also chose that name for the new East German carrier. The first official flight operated by Il-14 DDR-ABZ took off from Schönefeld on September 16, 1955, flying a government delegation including Walter Ulbricht to Moscow to sign the state treaty between GDR and Soviet Union. On this flight, and for months of the new airline's operation, only the passengers were German. Flight crews were "borrowed" from the Soviet Union until the airline was able to recruit and train their own pilots. Scheduled flights from the GDR began in spring 1956, with flights from Berlin to Warsaw, followed by occasional flights to Leipzig for the important Leipzig Trade Fair and service to Prague, Budapest, Sofia and Bucharest.

So while the name Lufthansa had been around since 1926, the Lufthansas before and after were effectively different companies.

In January 1956, the GDR filed their application to the patent authorities to use the Deutsche Lufthansa name and logo; the West Germans had already done so one and a half years earlier. With a decision pending (but the possible outcome quite clear), they kept on using the Deutsche Lufthansa name in the meantime and for some years, both East and West Germany had their own Deutsche Lufthansa, two airlines operating under the same name even though they had nothing to do with each other.

Deutsche Lufthansa in West Germany, henceforth Lufthansa FRG, was, of course, not very happy about another airline operating under the name they considered their property, having paid to use it, and the tense political situation between both Germanys did not help in solving this situation amicably. Lufthansa FRG lobbied hard to deny its East German counterpart the membership in international organisations or gain international traffic rights (mutual overflight rights were another matter, which remained unsolved pretty much until the fall of the Berlin Wall).

The GDR government was quite aware of the situation and that their opponent was in a much stronger position,

Il-14 resting between flights in front of the old terminal at Berlin Schönefeld
Page 10:
Mechanics working on the Shvetsov ASh-82T-7 engine of the Il-14
Interflug Abteilung Werbung

The Ilyushin Il-18 was only in Deutsche Lufthansa service for a short time before the GDR's airline became Interflug
Interflug Abteilung Werbung

should there be a legal dispute over the name and trademark rights, simply as they officially registered the name with the authorities much earlier. Even a GDR court would probably have ruled in favour of the FRG carrier in this case, so clear was the matter. Mostly to have a Plan B in the back pocket, a second East German airline was founded in September 1958 and officially registered as Interflug.

Primarily a charter airline (for example to the Leipzig trade fair), Interflug co-existed with Deutsche Lufthansa GDR for some years. As an airline, it was not really needed, as aircraft for charter missions were sourced from mainline anyway and the name and logo change was affected by the use of stickers. Interflug's importance lay in its function as a body for a new airline, should the dispute over the Deutsche Lufthansa name escalate.

When Deutsche Lufthansa FRG filed a suit over the name and trademark rights with the Higher Economic Court in Belgrade, the GDR government accepted the fact that it did not stand much of a chance in this case, agreed to liquidate its Deutsche Lufthansa and to continue under the Interflug name. On September 1, 1963, the transition was complete. Even though most of the assets such as aircraft, other infrastructure and traffic rights as well as staff were inherited from Deutsche Lufthansa GDR, Interflug was the name that survived and that was the airline that was to become the flag carrier for the GDR for the next decades.

The Ilyushin Il-14: the first people mover

The Ilyushin Il-14 was the aircraft with which Interflug's history began. After the Second World War, all civilian flying by German airlines was banned for ten years under the terms of the 1945 surrender. This decree was intended to consolidate the demilitarisation of Germany and until 1955, only foreign airlines served routes to Germany. The ban was lifted in 1955, by which time both Germanys had made extensive preparations to relaunch a national airline. In West Germany, Deutsche Lufthansa received their first Convair CV-340s and got ready to re-start commercial passenger flights; meanwhile the other Deutsche Lufthansa was keenly expecting the delivery of their first aircraft, an Ilyushin Il-14.

The Il-14 had evolved from the Il-12, intended to be a capable replacement for the Douglas DC-3 and its license-built Soviet version, the Lisunov Li-2. While the fuselage of the Il-12 and -14 was identical, the Il-14 featured several huge improvements over the -12 including a newly-designed wing and broader tailfin giving much better aerodynamic performance under normal conditions and in particular during an engine failure. With more economical Shvetsov ASh-82T-7 engines, the Il-14 also had more range and could carry significantly more payload than its predecessor.

The first aircraft of the new variant took to the air on October 1, 1950, and by 1955, the type was well-established in airline service with Aeroflot. On July 30, 1955, the first Il-14 destined for East Germany, DDR-ABA (a registration worn by Interflug's first Airbus A310 decades later) touched down at Schönefeld Airport, flown by a Soviet crew under the command of Captain Uvarov. A historical event for the GDR! Having their own national airline meant a lot to this small country and was a symbol of sovereignty and independence.

But the launch was a slow one. While the training of maintenance crews and other ground staff proceded apace, finding German cockpit crews proved to be a major challenge. The first official Deutsche Lufthansa (East) flight with Il-14 DDR-ABA took off from Berlin Schönefeld on September 16, 1955, transporting a government delegation to Moscow to sign the state treaty between the GDR and the Soviet Union which effectively gave the GDR full sovereignty.

Three more Il-14s were delivered to Schönefeld before the end of 1955: DDR-ABF, DDR-ABX and DDR-ABZ. With its own aircraft, the new airline was ready to fly. Initially, the GDR wanted to train their crews independently, a plan which soon proved to be over-ambitious, at least at short notice. The GDR simply did not have a proper flying school that could train commercial pilots, and establishing one would take some time. An airport southeast of Berlin, Preschen, was used for most of the GDR-based flight training including both civilian and military crews.

But it took too long. The GDR leaders were unhappy and wanted to see their new airline up in the air and flying and ideally without depending on Soviet expertise, at least in the longer term. Meanwhile, with no alternative, to expedite the entry of the first German pilots into airline service, the first crews were sent to Ulyanovsk in the Soviet Union for training. Until the first German pilots were licensed, Soviet pilots did the flying for the GDR's Deutsche Lufthansa.

Sourcing and training flight attendants was a lot easier, and from the very first flights, German flight attendants were on board, usually accompanied by a translator to ensure communication with the Russian pilots. The first scheduled route for the new airline was from Berlin to Warsaw, and the inaugural flight took off in February 1956, and operated twice a week. This was followed by charter flights from Berlin to the spring fair in Leipzig a few weeks later.

Preparing for more international routes, Deutsche Lufthansa signed a revenue-sharing and sales agreement with the airlines of Bulgaria (TABSO), Czechoslovakia (CSA), Hungary (MALÉV) and Poland (LOT). May 1956 saw the opening of new routes to Prague, Budapest, Sofia and Bucharest, an ambitious expansion. Cockpit crews were mostly Russians; Deutsche Lufthansa's first Il-14 flight operated under the control of a German captain did not take place until March 1957, on the Berlin-Vilnius-Moscow route. More and more German cockpit crews were now licensed, and the

An Il-14 on final approach
Previous image: Deutsche Lufthansa Il-14

Interflug Abteilung Werbung

The Il-14s were sourced from several production plants, the USSR (DM-SB...) and Dresden (DM-SA...) Interflug Abteilung Werbung

same was true for certified maintenance staff, and the airline was able to run its operation more independently, something both its management and the GDR government were very keen on.

In 1956, GDR-registered aircraft changed their country code prefix from DDR- used initially to DM- (reversed in 1981 when the register went back to DDR-). With this change, DDR-ABA became DM-SBA, DDR-ABF was re-registered DM-SBF, DDR-ABX became DM-SBX, and DDR-ABZ became DM-SBZ.

At the same time as the state airline was launched, another, even more challenging project went ahead: the creation of a proper GDR aviation industry. The airport of Dresden was chosen as the site for a production plant, as some infrastructure and engineering knowledge was already there and could be taken advantage of. An agreement was signed with the Soviet Union to build 80 Il-14s under licence. After some delays that were not entirely unexpected, the first Dresden-built Ilyushin, registered DM-ZZC, was delivered to the GDR's National People's Army on April 30, 1957.

A few weeks later, on June 28, the next example was delivered to Deutsche Lufthansa, registered DM-SAA. With the first German-built Il-14 delivered, Deutsche Lufthansa had a total of ten ships in its fleet in summer 1957. One can distinguish Russian-built Il-14s from the GDR-built ones by their registration: those starting with DM-SB... were built in Russia, while those registered DM-SA... were Dresden-made.

The growing fleet allowed Deutsche Lufthansa to not only fly their growing programme of international routes but also launch its first domestic routes. On June 16, the first flight took off from Schönefeld to Barth, close to the Baltic Sea coast. On the same day, flights started from Berlin to Dresden and to Erfurt, which at the time only had a steel runway, later replaced by a longer concrete strip.

By the end of 1958, all 80 of the Il-14s to be built in Dresden had been completed, quite a smooth success story, most of them delivered to the National People's Army. Deutsche Lufthansa's Il-14 fleet reached a peak of 27 in

After retiring from Interflug service in 1968 this ship was converted into a calibration aircraft and served until 1984. Today it is on display at Dresden Airport**Jacques Guillem**

1960, most of them built locally. When Deutsche Lufthansa became Interflug, they were repainted into the new red and white scheme, although some of them remained in the Deutsche Lufthansa colours and just had their titles changed. After the initial delays (which were not the aircraft's fault), the Il-14 did a good job building Interflug's domestic and European network, and both passengers and crews (three in the cockpit and a single flight attendant) liked the sturdy aircraft. With the arrival of the much bigger and capable Ilyushin Il-18 and later the Antonov An-24s, the Il-14 fleet started to shrink. Most aircraft were passed on to the military forces of friendly countries like Syria or Egypt and ended their days there. The last Il-14 was eventually retired from service with Interflug in 1967. It had served its purpose well.

Three Dresden-built Il-14s remain on display today: DM-SAF was number 16 off the Dresden production line and delivered to Deutsche Lufthansa in December 1957. Not even ten years later, it was written off after a hard landing in Leipzig. After years of storage and in increasingly deteriorating condition, it was transferred to the Hugo Junkers Museum in Dessau, where the aircraft was carefully refurbished and painted into contemporary Deutsche Lufthansa colours. It is still on display in front of the museum today and in very good condition.

DM-SAL was another Il-14 that flew with Deutsche Lufthansa. Delivered in March 1958, it flew commercially for a good ten years, before Interflug briefly used it as a training aircraft. As the Il-14 fleet was retired from service soon after, the airline no longer had any use for it and it was converted to a calibration aircraft servicing the GDR's navigational aids from then on. In 1984, DDR-SAL (it had been re-registered) was retired and replaced as a calibration aircraft by Il-18 DDR-STP. A year after its retirement, it was flown to Dresden where it is still on display today, wearing Deutsche Lufthansa colours and its original registration DM-SAL.

DM-SAB is the third aircraft that is still around today, preserved in full Interflug colours and parked outside the village of Caemmerswalde, close to the Czech border, in good condition.

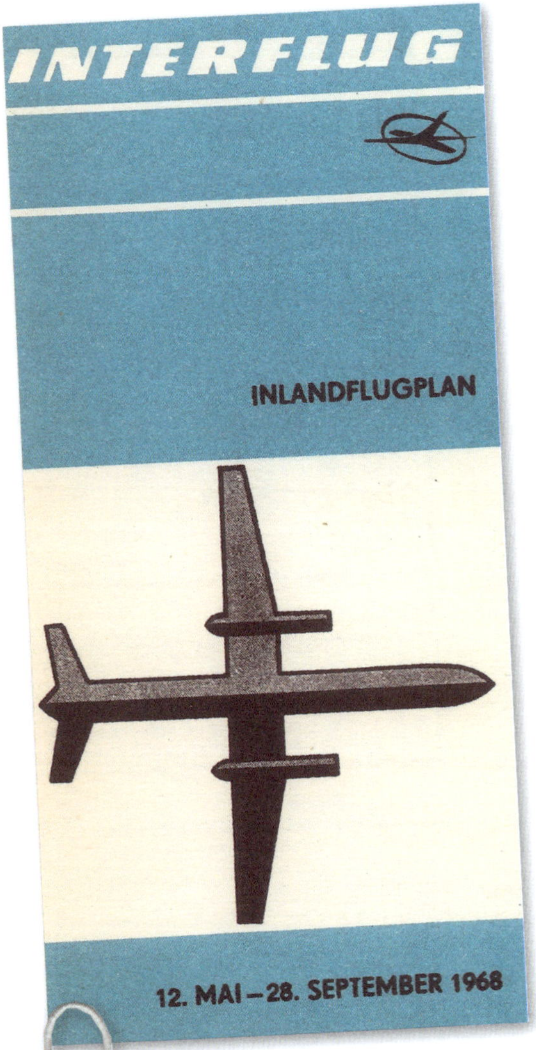

INTERFLUG
INLANDFLUGPLAN
12. MAI – 28. SEPTEMBER 1968

BORDKARTE
ПОСАДОЧНЫЙ ТАЛОН
BOARDING PASS
Flug-Nr.
№ рейса
Flight-No.
620
Reihe Nr.
№ ряда
Row-No.
12
X
Für IL-14 ist die Sitznummer eingetragen
Для самолета ИЛ-14 записывается номера кресель
For the IL-14 aircraft the seat-numbers are indicated
BUDAPEST

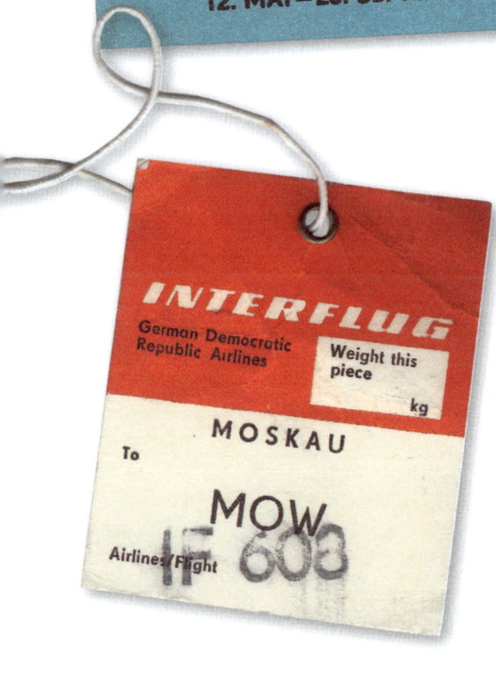

INTERFLUG
German Democratic Republic Airlines
Weight this piece
kg
MOSKAU
To
MOW
Airlines/Flight
IF 603

LUFTPOST · PAR AVION
INTERFLUG
LUFTPOST · PAR AVION
INTERFLUG
LUFTPOST · PAR AVION
INTERFLUG
LUFTPOST · PAR AVION
INTERFLUG
LUFTPOST · PAR AVION
INTERFLUG

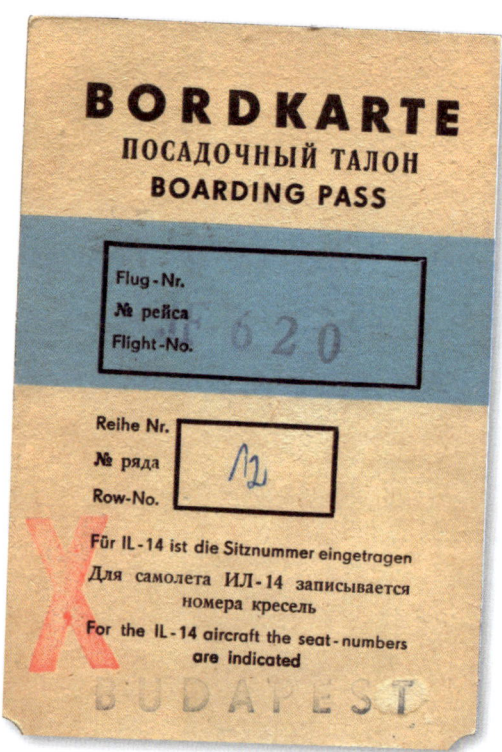

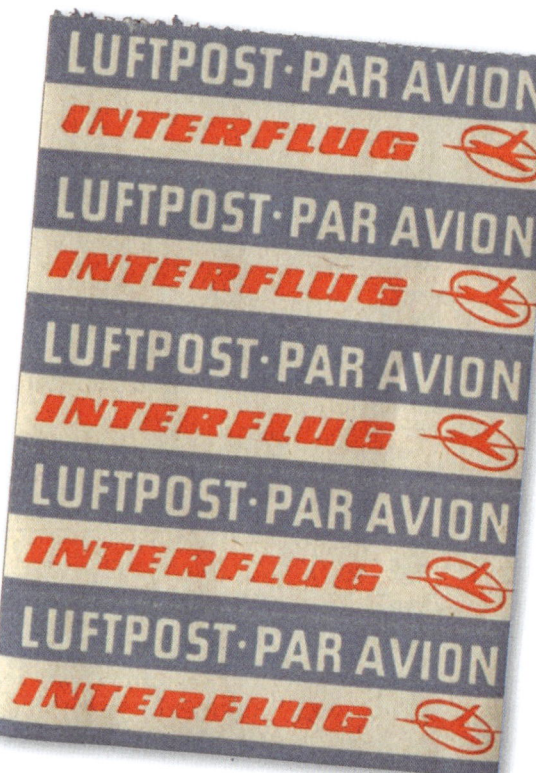

The Antonov An-24 and GDR domestic flying

One aircraft type in Interflug's fleet that was not a success was the Antonov An-24, even though it was only partly the aircraft's fault. With its robust design and high wings, the An-24, which was given the nickname Duck, seemed like the perfect aircraft for Interflug to replace the smaller and somewhat limited Ilyushin Il-14 (of which Interflug had up to 27) on domestic and shorter regional flights. And for a time, it was.

The first five An-24s, DM-SBA, -SBC, -SBD, -SBE and -SBF, were all delivered to Interflug in the space of a few weeks in the spring of 1966, with a sixth following in early 1967. The introduction of the type, and the replacement of the Il-14, was prepared meticulously.

With just a few exceptions where pilots had to be borrowed from the Soviet Union temporarily, Interflug's own crews were trained in time and the An-24's introduction into service was smooth. The first route for the Duck was Berlin-Warsaw, with the inaugural flight taking to the air on April 1, 1966. The turboprop soon took over all domestic flights and some shorter regional routes.

At the time, the domestic network was quite impressive for a country as small as the GDR, and included Dresden, Erfurt and Leipzig year-round, with summer trips to Barth and Heringsdorf, both close to the GDR's Baltic Sea coast. Some shorter and thinner international routes were also flown by the An-24 including Budapest, Bratislava, Copenhagen, Krakow, Tatry, Vienna, Stockholm and Warsaw.

While many airlines seemed overly happy with the type (and the fact that the An-24 is still operated by numerous carriers today is proof of that), Interflug never really warmed to the aircraft and financial results were one reason; the domestic routes in particular generated heavy losses and even though the An-24 was probably the right size to operate them (certainly more suitable than any other type in the fleet), it was not efficient enough to improve the numbers. In retrospect, the type can be called a misfit, at least for the GDR carrier.

Crews who flew the An-24 liked the type. With its low service ceiling and speed, it was a bit like travelling by bus. When the weather was nice, the sightseeing could be excellent. When the weather was less clement, things could get rather bumpy because of the low altitude the An-24 travelled at, but nothing could impress this sturdy plane. And the open hat racks were perfect for the flight attendant to hold on to when things got bumpy!

While the cockpit crew consisted of three, the flight attendant worked in the cabin by her- or himself, taking care of up to 48 passengers. This was sometimes quite stressful but when flights were not full, there was usually a quite familiar

Antonov An-24B DM-SBF at Brussels Airport in July 1972
Previous page: DM-SBF seen at Copenhagen Airport in July 1970
Page 20: The An-24 was the workhorse on Interflug's domestic network and also used for shorter international flights.

Guy Viselé
Jacques Guillem

atmosphere on board. Even with flights being short, the crews often had quite long working days. Flying six domestic segments was not unheard of, and often resulted in duty times of ten hours or more. A trip of six legs could look like Berlin-Barth-Leipzig-Heringsdorf-Leipzig-Barth-Berlin. Domestic trips also included the occasional layover for the crews to be in position to operate an early morning departure back to Berlin, or ground transport between airports by road.

Domestic flying saw its peak in 1969, when more than 250,000 passengers travelled on Interflug services within the GDR. Even though these flights were loss-making, ambitious plans existed to bring the number of passengers up to 700,000 or even 900,000 by 1975 with an upgraded airport in Heringsdorf and entirely new airports in Karl-Marx-Stadt (today Chemnitz) and Rostock.

An unrealistic dream. In fact, with road connections getting better, rising car ownership, and greatly improved connections between the GDR's major cities by Deutsche Reichsbahn trains, Interflug's short domestic flights had less and less advantage over other means of transport. Even with fully booked flights (and this was also true for the bigger Ilyushin Il-18, which was also used on domestic sectors), the operational costs remained high, even more so as fuel costs rose.

Thus, even though politically desirable, the domestic network became increasingly unloved by management, and increasingly neglected. When there was an operational delay or technical problem, more profitable international flights were always given priority, leading to numerous domestic cancellations and delays. Increasing unreliability did not endear Interflug's domestic network to potential travellers, creating a vicious circle. Thus, instead of domestic passenger numbers growing as planned, things went downhill, and in 1973, there were only 77,000 travellers on Interflug services within the GDR.

The somewhat unloved An-24 was phased out of the Interflug fleet in 1976, also in an effort to have fewer aircraft types in the fleet. The much bigger but also more efficient Il-18 (at least when carrying a full load) replaced it on the surviving domestic sectors, and a mix of Il-18 and Tu-134 on international flights. The short career of the An-24 with Interflug, around a decade of service, came to an end. The six flying for Interflug (DM-SBA, -SBC, -SBD, -SBE, -SBF and -SBG) were retired almost simultaneously in 1976. A seventh aircraft, DM-SBH, was operated on behalf of the Ministry of State Security, although, like most of the aircraft operating for the Stasi or other government institutions, wore Interflug colours. 'BH was retired a year later, in 1977.

All aircraft were given a proper overhaul in Kiev and six of them passed on to Vietnam as a gift of solidarity to a fellow communist nation, joining Hang Khong Viet Nam, today Vietnam Airlines. The first one to fly with Interflug, DM-SBA, was sold to Balkan Bulgarian Airlines as LZ-ANL. It is the only known survivor of the seven, today part of a small aviation museum at Burgas Airport in Bulgaria in all-white colours.

A few years after the An-24s were gone, on March 27, 1980, the Council of Ministers decided to abandon domestic flights entirely, a reluctant but probably inevitable decision and one that was preceded by significant cuts to the network and the frequency of flights. Domestic flights within the GDR stopped just two weeks later, on April 10. Interflug, however, continued operating flights from other airports than Berlin, mostly Leipzig and Dresden, but these flights were all international (such as to Budapest, Sofia, Moscow or the resorts at the Black Sea) and were usually flown in W-patterns originating in Schönefeld.

IF

A small excursion by train

The Antonov An-24 had a rather short career with Interflug. While the airline never really fell in love with the type, the GDR's much improved railway network and consequently the cessation of domestic flights were what really ended the An-24's career with Interflug. I hope, even though this is an aviation book, you don't mind a short excursion to the country's railway system.

Before World War Two (and the partition of the country), railway lines in Germany were operated by Deutsche Reichsbahn. The train network was quite comprehensive, connecting even the most remote corners of the country to its main cities.

After the end of the war, Germany was divided and that was also true for its railway system. Unlike civilian flying, which only started again in 1955, railway lines were reinstated quite quickly, once the tracks and other infrastructure was sufficiently repaired to allow services to run.

In East Germany, then occupied by the Soviets, the railway company continued operating as Deutsche Reichsbahn. The story seems to resemble that of the Deutsche Lufthansa brand, which was used in both Germanys for a while. Unlike Deutsche Lufthansa name, which the GDR had to give up, this time it was the GDR that kept the name of what was once the all-German railway operator. In West Germany, the new name of the railway company was Deutsche Bundesbahn.

Even though damage to the network was quite significant, operations were reduced further in the immediate aftermath of the war. The Soviet Union claimed huge reparations in both money and materiel, including important items of the rail infrastructure which were ripped up and taken to the Soviet Union to help build and improve the railway network there. This included actual tracks, reducing most lines to just a single track except for the main line between Frankfurt-Oder, Berlin, Leipzig and Erfurt. (Some of it was returned later in exchange for the delivery of several hundred train wagons built in the GDR).

Once the GDR became an independent country, one of the most urgent railway projects was the construction of a ring around West Berlin so that trains originating in the Eastern part could avoid transiting the Western part of the city.

Even though most of the network was hobbled by being single-track one way streets, the railways of the GDR were quite comprehensive. For most of the GDR's existence, Deutsche Reichsbahn was the country's biggest employer, with around 250,000 employees, which was a lot in a country of 16 or 17 million people.

Most of the cargo and goods transported around the country – in some years as much as 85% – went by rail, unlike in West Germany, where most was driven around by truck (as is the case today).

An important reason for East Germany to stick with the Deutsche Reichsbahn was to retain its operating rights in West Berlin. With the approval of the Western Allies, the entire network of suburban trains (S-Bahn) in West Berlin was operated by the GDR until 1984. As these operating rights had been granted to "Deutsche Reichsbahn" and was important to the GDR government to have a foot in the door of West Berlin, they were afraid of the consequences of a name change. Although the S-Bahn was once the most popular way to get around town, many West Berliners boycotted it because of the operator (and were encouraged by politicians to do so). They saw buying a fare as paying a subsidy to the GDR. And the BVG, the transit company of West Berlin, immediately started opening bus lines and later subway lines which often ran parallel to the S-Bahn tracks. Service and tracks declined until in January 9, 1984, when the responsibility for operating the Western half of the S-Bahn network was handed to BVG, ending one of the many absurdities in this divided city. Following this transfer, much of the network was restored and people started using its trains once more.

What was truly revolutionary was the introduction of the so-called Städte-Express in 1976. The introduction of the new trains happened somewhat by accident. In 1976, Czechoslovakia was unable to take delivery of over 100 newly-built passenger coaches from the GDR because of financing problems. This gave Deutsche Reichsbahn the chance to take over a significant number of brand new passenger cars at short notice, giving much needed extra capacity at the time and providing a top notch travel experience compared to previous

Night time scene at Berlin's Ostbahnhof
Previous image: Busy times at Leipzig railway station in 1981

Dr. Uwe Knoblauch
Karsten Risch

The Städte-Express was the flagship of the GDR's rail network   Ralf Opalka

models. Luckily, most of the country's main rail lines had been electrified just a few months earlier. The new rolling stock was conspicuously painted and off they went into service.

From autumn 1976, the Städte-Express (or City Express) connected most major cities in the GDR with Berlin, with early morning departures to Berlin and evening returns back from the capital. Even though they didn't go much faster than previous trains (the maximum speed was 120 km/h, not exactly supersonic), they stopped less often and were given priority over other trains. And to be fair the GDR was not a very large country, so if you travelled at 120 km/h for a while, you covered a large portion of the country in fairly short order.

As the trains were mostly used by business people or party officials (there was a surcharge to use it) they were soon given the loving nickname "Bonzenschleuder" by the rest of the population, which would roughly translate into "Fatcat shuttle" in English. Because of the important audience often travelling in these trains, the restaurant cars – every train had one – often had items available (such as certain brands of beer) that were sold out in regular shops. Every train service had its own particular name and, contrary to what one might maybe expect, they were not called "Vladimir I. Lenin" or "Walter Ulbricht" but quite romantic names such as "Elbflorenz" (the nickname of Dresden), "Berliner Bär" (after the bear that is the heraldic animal of Berlin) or "Lipsia" (the Latin name of Leipzig). When more trains became available and the tracks were improved, additional frequencies were added, with most lines also seeing morning departures from Berlin.

With the reunification of the two Germanys, Deutsche Reichsbahn was merged with Deutsche Bundesbahn to form an all-German railway company once more. In 1994, both companies ceased to exist and formed Deutsche Bahn. Many of the engines that were inherited from the GDR are still in use with Deutsche Bahn today. If you feel like seeing a Städte-Express carriage, freshly painted in the contemporary bright orange, you should visit the railway museum in Leipzig. They occasionally even take it on nostalgic train tours, together with other vintage GDR carriages and engines.

The Baade 152: a homegrown jetliner

When writing about the airline of the GDR, it is definitely worth mentioning an aircraft type that is hardly known today and for which Interflug (still known as Deutsche Lufthansa at that time) was expected to become an important customer: the Baade 152, a GDR-built passenger jet.

Let me reach back a little bit: after the end of World War Two, with Germany in ruins, the scientific elite of the country was looking for career opportunities outside of Germany: aircraft and rocket engineers, engine constructors or aerodynamicists. Many ended up in the United States, but for those living in the Soviet-occupied Eastern sector of Germany, the destination was often the Soviet Union. About 3,000 of them were brought to the Soviet Union in 1946, probably not all voluntarily, where their expertise was used for military and aviation projects.

One of these was former Junkers engineer (the planemaker most famous for its Junkers Ju-52), Brunolf Baade. During his time in the Soviet Union, he worked on a shoulder-wing jet engine bomber called the "150". After some test flights of the protoype and a serious landing accident in May 1953, the project was abandoned in favour of the Soviets' own design, the Tu-16 bomber.

The German engineers were not really needed any longer and allowed to return to the GDR, but at the same time, the Soviets and the GDR government were afraid to lose them and the knowledge they carried around in their heads to the enemy, the West. Thus, a proper GDR-based aircraft construction sector was secretly set up. The main motivation was for the economic benefit and prestige of mastering high tech industries, but retaining highly skilled workers played a role.

Plans included the production under license of the MiG-15 at the former Junkers plant in Dessau. After the anti-government uprising of June 17, 1953 in the GDR, the Soviet Union abandoned the project, wary of a technology transfer to a potentially unreliable ally. The GDR government still wanted to continue with the creation of its own GDR aviation industry, whether it made economic sense or not. This time around, the region of Saxony was chosen as the homebase of this new high-tech industrial sector. An engine factory was built in the town of Pirna and the main production and development plant of what was called the VEB Flugzeugwerke Dresden (roughly translates as "People Owned Company Aircraft Factory Dresden") found a home at Dresden Airport, with state-of-the-art design offices and laboratories, test stands and a wind tunnel as well as production halls.

Equipment for this new industry, quite ironically, was often sourced from the West against hard currency. A lot of money and effort was invested into this showcase industry, more than this little country could probably afford at the time, but the project had the full support of the government and Walter Ulbricht, the First Secretary of the Socialist Unity Party of the GDR and the country's chief decision maker at the time, and quite enthusiastic about aviation.

So here was a flashy new factory with a lot of talent in need of a project: the construction of the first German jet airliner, the four-engine Baade 152. A team under Brunolf Baade set out to convert the Bomber 150, designed during their time in the Soviet Union, into a civilian passenger jet. Some bomber features were retained, such as the glazed nose with navigator seat, the tandem main landing gear with additional support wheels under the wing tips, and the engines now mounted in twin nacelles under the arrowed wings.

The initial design of this new aircraft would have been able to carry 24 passengers at 700 to 750 kmh (435 to 465 mph) over distances of 2,500 kilometres (1,553 miles), able to take off from a 1,000 metre (3,281 foot) runway. During several design updates, the number of passengers was first increased to 40 and later from 48 up to 72, depending on seat configuration.

Before production of the Baade 152 started and in order to get everyone acquainted to building a larger number of aircraft, the plant started assembling Ilyushin Il-14P piston propliners under license from the Soviets, and producing glider aircraft before the prototype of the Baade 152 was built.

The project had to become a success and the pressure on everyone involved was immense. On April 30, 1958, a day before the important May 1st celebrations, the roll-out of the first Baade 152 took place, witnessed by Walter

The 152/I V4 rolls out of the production hall 222 in Dresden-Klotzsche
Previous image: The 152/I V1 during taxi tests in December 1958

Flugzeug-Lorenz.de

An Il-14 is used as a flying test bed for the Baade 152's horizontal stabiliser
Flugzeug-Lorenz.de

Ulbricht. As is often the case with the unveiling of new aircraft types, especially when working to an artificial timeline (May Day), essential parts of the equipment (and the engines) were still missing.

The first flight of the prototype took to the air half a year later, on December 4, 1958, and lasted roughly half an hour. Because of problems with the fuel system that needed to be fixed, three months passed before the second flight took place March 1959. Commercial pressure was unabated: the aircraft was to be presented at the Leipzig Spring Fair, a very important event for the GDR industry where its products were not only presented to socialist brother countries but also to potential customers from the West. And this aircraft urgently needed customers!

The GDR put high hopes in non-binding declarations of interest from the Soviet Union for up to 100 aircraft. The Baade 152 was to be flown to Leipzig for the event, which was attended by Walter Ulbricht and Nikita Khrushchev. But the aircraft never got there: while on approach to Dresden Airport for a low pass with retracted flaps and landing gear, it crashed some four miles short of the runway, killing all four onboard.

The accident report partly blames the crew for the crash, having performed an unusually steep climb up to 6,000 metres (19,685 feet), followed by a very steep descent, both beyond the specified climb and descent rates. This could have caused previously known problems with the ventilation of the rubber tank cells and float valves. It was an aerodynamic stall that caused the jetliner to go out of control and crash but the initiating reasons that led to the accident was never determined beyond doubt.

This accident did not make the overall pressure on the project any less; expectations were high and the project team now almost three years behind schedule. Prototype number four was made ready for its maiden flight, this time powered by the GDR-built Pirna 014A-0 engines instead of Soviet-built ones. DM-ZYB took off on its maiden flight on August 26, 1960, followed by a second sortie in September. But these flights and further tests on the ground revealed severe ongoing design deficiencies in the aircraft's fuel system.

As it was not deemed fully safe to fly, the 152's flight approval was revoked by the authorities until significant upgrades could be presented. Prototype number three, registered DM-ZYC, had been completed but never made it beyond high-speed tests on the ground. It never flew.

The scale of the production line at Dresden illustrates the ambition of the Baade 152 project
via Historical.Aviation (Instagram)

The only remaining fuselage of a Baade 152 is on display at Dresden Airport.
Luftfahrtarchiv Matthias Winkler

This is what a Baade 152 would have looked like in Deutsche Lufthansa colours. **Flugzeug-Lorenz.de**

In early 1961, it looked like flight testing could resume once more by the end of the year. But with the Soviet Union officially declaring that it was no longer interested in the aircraft and no other customers in sight, commercial prospects for the aircraft looked very dire. Russian designs like the Tupolev Tu-104 and Tu-124 were already flying and with the Tu-134 already on the horizon, there was no prize to be won with what was an interesting but ultimately inferior design. The only potential customers in sight were Deutsche Lufthansa (GDR) and the GDR's National People's Army, with a demand of up to 30 aircraft expected from each – not enough to continue with this already severely delayed project.

In February 1961, the Politbüro of the GDR decided to discontinue aircraft production in the GDR and abandon this project. The order was issued to scrap all completed and partly-assembled aircraft and their parts, probably in order to not display what was ultimately a huge failure for the GDR government, in public. Some twelve aircraft were fully or partly assembled at the time. In practice some of them escaped scrapping at first and were used for decades at East German airports as equipment sheds or for fire brigade training.

Only one fuselage, serial number 011, was accidentally preserved at the airport of Rothenburg, salvaged after the end of the GDR and restored, now on display at Dresden Airport. The production halls at Dresden Airport were used for non-aeronautical purposes for decades – agricultural machines and bob sleighs were produced here, among other things.

It was only after the fall of the Berlin Wall that aircraft construction was taken up once more. Elbe Flugzeugwerke was born, and has become a success story. Initially a supplier of tail sections for Dutch planemaker Fokker, it later specialized in the conversion of passenger aircraft to freighters, most of them Airbus A300-600s. Today a part of Airbus, Elbe Flugzeugwerke has started conversion of Airbus A330s to freighters and will do so in the future with A320s and 321s. It has also performed maintenance on several Airbus A380s.

The Baade 152 never made it beyond just a few flights, let alone into commercial service, and the entire project to set up their own aircraft industry probably cost the GDR billions. However it is good to know that at least one (partial) Baade 152 has survived until this day and that Dresden has become a flourishing location for the aviation industry, decades after the last aircraft was built there.

The Ilyushin Il-18: long haul turboprop

The four-engined Ilyushin Il-18 served Interflug the longest of any type, covering almost the entire existence of the airline. 31 years passed between the delivery of the first Il-18 to Deutsche Lufthansa and the retirement of the last Il-18 from Interflug service (well, the entire airline stopped flying). To compare this to the other main types Interflug operated: the Tu-134 lasted 23 years, the Il-62 21 years, the Il-14 12 years and the An-24 a surprisingly short seven years. That the Il-18s flew on after the demise of Interflug for Berline under Western, 'commercial' conditions shows the type's versatility, its ability to operate in many different roles and reasonably efficiently.

There are actually two different aircraft designs called the 'Ilyushin Il-18'. The original made its first flight on August 17, 1946 (hey, August 17 is the editor's birthday). It was quite an advanced design, with four piston engines, a pressurized cabin and retractable landing gear. Even though test flights were quite promising, design and production capacity was needed elsewhere and an aircraft this size, at least for now, was not really needed until the middle of the 1950s, when Aeroflot demanded a larger aircraft that could carry between 75 and 100 passengers on short and medium haul routes. The Il-18 was taken back out of the drawer and the initial design was used as the basis for what is actually the Il-18 V2.0. The first flight took off from Moscow's Khodinka Airport on July 4, 1957 (hey, July 4 is the author's birthday). With different versions and upgrades over the years, the Il-18 became quite a hit not only with Aeroflot but also with airlines abroad and the fact that some are still operating today underlines what a sturdy aircraft this is.

Before the arrival of the Il-18, the aircraft that Interflug's operation depended upon was the much smaller piston-driven Il-14, an aircraft that worked on shorter sectors such as Berlin to Prague or Warsaw or on domestic flights, but definitely reached a limit on longer routes such as Sofia, Bucharest, Vilnius or Moscow which were all served in 1959, just before the first Il-18 arrived. The plan was to have two Il-18s join the fleet in the first quarter of 1960, with third joining in the third quarter. Already in 1959, the first crews went to Aeroflot's flying college in Ulyanovsk to receive their training on the type and an Il-18 squadron was founded within Interflug, typical for the mIlitary-oriented organization of the airline.

After slight delays, the first Il-18, DM-STA, was delivered to Schönefeld on March 28, 1960, still flown by an Aeroflot flight crew and bringing some instructors to Berlin to further train local crews on type. It was followed by DM-STB soon after and the Il-18 almost immediately entered commercial service

During the transition from Deutsche Lufthansa to Interflug some aircraft wore hybrid colours
Previous image: Ivchenko AI-20M turbine driven props ready to fly
Interflug Abteilung Werbung

on the prestigious route to Moscow on April 3. On the Moscow route, the new turbine-powered type better than halved the flight time (the Il-14 typically needed an intermediate stop in Vilnius en route) and more than doubled the number of passenger seats compared to the Il-14. Quite a step!

By the middle of July, all three Il-18s were delivered but because of technical bugs, they saw the maintenance hangar more than they flew and frequently had to go back to Moscow for overhaul. Luckily, most of the Il-14s were still there as backup planes and these sturdy old workhorses were able to make up for some of the cancelled flights because of spontaneous maintenance events. Even though they were quite maintenance-prone, too, the fleet of Il-14s was quite large at almost 30 ships and aircraft availability was not as much of an issue as it was with the much smaller Il-18 fleet.

While the introduction of the Il-18 on the prestigious Moscow route was a major development, competitor Aeroflot was always one step ahead. They sent the first jet aircraft, the Tu-104, to Schönefeld for a visit in July 1961, and regularly deployed the type on the Berlin route beginning the following year. Thus, just as Interflug was able to offer their passengers an improved experience with the introdcution of the Il-18 on flights to Moscow, Aeroflot offered jet service! With a shorter flight time and a higher level of comfort, most passengers that had a choice gave Aeroflot their preference, a situation Interflug had to deal with until the introduction of their first jet aircraft, the Tu-134 in 1968.

Adding to the somewhat bumpy introduction of the Il-18, the political situation was very uncertain at the time (1961 was the year the Berlin wall was built) and the GDR was quite isolated internationally. Even though the Il-18 had the capabilities to start a whole new range of destinations, many of them remained beyond Interflug's reach because of the febrile political

situation at the time. This only started to change as more countries recognised the GDR, and relations with West Germany changed from very tense and adversarial to a more pragmatic footing.

In the summer of 1961, the Il-18 started the first holiday flights to the Black Sea resorts of Varna in Bulgaria and Constanta in Romania, a mission it was quite well-suited for with its range and size. In 1962, Leningrad became one of the first destinations for the type, and in spring 1963, it operated a series of charter flights from Leipzig for the trade fair there, a hugely important event in the GDR and Interflug calendar.

Indeed of all the aircraft Interflug ever operated, the Il-18 had the widest mission profile by far, be it a short hop to the GDR's Baltic Sea coast or a week-long government trip to Asia. It had the range to operate long haul flights, the capability to land on even the most short or ill-equipped runways, was easy to use on either passenger or cargo missions.

One major mission took place in February 1964, flying a government delegation to Indonesia, Cambodia, Burma, Sri Lanka and India, including the first equator crossing of an Il-18 in Interflug service. While it was always an important and quite flexible part of Interflug's scheduled network, special missions became the 'second home' for the Il-18 fleet. In 1964 and 1965 alone, solidarity flights brought the Il-18 to Mongolia after a natural disaster there, as well as solidarity flights to Yemen, Cyprus and Vietnam.

At the same time, the Interflug network continued to grow and new routes were opened using the Il-18, such as to Cairo, or on a very peculiar route from Berlin to Conakry in Guinea via Algiers, and Bamako in Mali. By the middle of the 1970s, the fleet had grown to an impressive 15 ships, leaving plenty of room operationally to fly scheduled routes as well as special missions. And that could also be regular charter flights, such as flying fresh vegetables from Italy

Delivered to the GDR in September 1962, this ship served its entire life with Interflug until retirement on November 24, 1989, fifteen days after the fall of the Berlin wall and was flown to Borkheide in 1990 where it is on display today
Jacques Guillem

to Sweden. Whatever that brought into the GDR as hard currency was quite welcome! In 1977, an Interflug Il-18 crossed the Atlantic for the first time, again on a special mission, flying much-needed vaccines to Argentina.

And not only did GDR officials often use it, whenever needed, but aircraft capacity was also loaned to befriended fellow socialist states. And that could be operating scheduled flights on behalf of Czechoslovakia's CSA Airlines for a few weeks, taking a Vietnamese delegation on a government trip around Africa, or picking up the president of Cape Verde and his entourage for a state visit to the GDR. The Il-18's life never got dull while it flew for Interflug! A load of school books to Kabul, baby chickens to Baghdad, picking up orphans in Angola, bringing wounded PLO fighters from Yemen to the GDR for treatment, the Il-18 did it all.

And it was an important tool in GDR foreign politics. With the arrival of the first Il-62s in 1970, the Il-18's role started to change. Most long haul routes were eventually moved to the Il-62 and the Il-18 was downgraded from being Interflug's flagship to busier routes around Europe such as to Moscow, Leningrad or Budapest or holiday charters, often on behalf of tour operators from West Germany, where the aircraft's capacity came in handy and range was sufficient to reach most places around the Mediterranean or Black Sea.

Special missions and charter flights remained as important as ever. In March 1989 an Interflug Il-18 flew to Toulouse, bringing crews there for their conversion training on the soon to be delivered Airbus A310. What a step, converting from a steam age Il-18 to a fly-by-wire Airbus A310! Over the years, Interflug's Il-18s landed at 212 different airports in 87 countries and five continents, quite an impressive proof of the hugely important role the type played for both Interflug and the GDR.

After the end of commercial flying for Interflug (and the end of Interflug itself), some members of the Il-18 squadron founded a small airline called Il-18 Air Cargo, soon renamed as Berline. The airline took over five Il-18s and flew them on passenger and cargo charters, not without some success. The Il-18s operated in a blue, white and grey colour scheme that was definitely inspired by the early Deutsche Lufthansa colours. The Il-18s that were not donated to museums went on to fly with often dubious carriers in Kazakhstan, Kyrgyzstan, Angola or Cuba and none remain in operation today. It is safe to say that without the Il-18, Interflug would not have accomplished nearly as much.

Interflug Abteilung Werbung

A number of Il-18s have survived to this day and during the editing of this book, very happy news reached us from Erfurt, where after years of storage, DDR-STG was recently repainted in full Interflug colours and will be used as a 'flying classroom', teaching school kids about environmental issues once its interior is fully refurbished. Another Il-18 survivor in very good condition and the only one wearing full "Deutsche Lufthansa" colours is DM-STA, the first one delivered to Interflug. It is in splendid condition (at least from outside) and parked right in front of the passenger terminal at Leipzig Airport, very easy to see and photograph. DDR-STB is wearing full Interflug colours and graces the roof of the Da Capo oldtimer museum and event hall in Leipzig. Other than just decorating it, the aircraft does not have a function there but as of summer 2019, it was in rather good condition at least from outside. DDR-STD has found new use as a luxury hotel suite at the airfield of Teuge in the Netherlands, wearing white and grey Hotelsuites colours, www.hotelsuites.nl. DDR-STE was flown from Schönefeld to the tiny airfield of Borkheide, southwest of Berlin, on November 16, 1989, and landed on the short grass runway there. Ever since, it has been the star of the Hans Grade Museum and can be visited without appointment during the summer months and by appointment in the winter. As is mostly the case, small private initiatives are short of cash most of the time. A much-needed repaint of the aircraft has not taken place yet but will hopefully happen in the coming years. DDR-STG, as mentioned earlier, has just been repainted at Erfurt Airport and its future seems secure. The last survivor in Interflug colours, DDR-STH, is preserved in the Flugausstellung Junior in the town of Hermeskeil, southwest Germany. It is wearing full Interflug colours and joins Tupolev 134 DDR-SCK, which is also part of the exhibition.

The Tupolev Tu-134: jet power at last

The first Soviet-built jet airliner, and the first in the world to manage sustained service, the Tupolev Tu-104 was a design masterpiece and showed the world that Soviet Union industry was capable of matching, or bettering, what the West could do. Aeroflot used the Tu-104 quite extensively on medium haul routes, with the giant prop-powered Tu-114 used on long haul flights. The Yakovlev Yak-40 was a jet suitable for short and thin routes, but there was a need to develop a capable jet between those two, a 60 or 70 seater. That was the Tupolev Tu-124, a smaller and lighter Tu-104 derivative, with three delivered to the GDR and operated by the country's armed forces, albeit two of them in Interflug colours. Other than as an occasional substitute on Interflug flights, they never entered commercial service in the country.

The Tu-104 and -124 had their two engines mounted in the wing root right alongside the fuselage, making for a very noisy passenger experience. Soviet premier Nikita Khrushchev flew on a Sud Aviation Caravelle at the Paris Air Show in 1960, which had engines mounted on the rear fuselage, and was so impressed by the quiet cabin during flight that upon his return he ordered engineers to build a jet with the same configuration.

During the design of what would become the Tupolev Tu-134, many features of the Tu-124 were retained, including the fuselage, wing and landing gear. The first Tu-134 took off for the first time on July 29, 1963, and with more than 850 aircraft following it down the line at the factory in Kharkiv (today Ukraine, then the Ukrainian SSR of the Soviet Union). There were almost 30 different versions and sub-versions, from the basic Tu-134 with only 64 seats, through the upgraded 134A and eventually the 134B-3 which could seat up to 96 passengers. NATO gave it the lovely nickname "Crusty", while Russians often referred to it as "Tushka", the "little Tu". The type was a success, operating in virtually all Warsaw Pact states and many friendly countries, including being Interflug's first jet type, although only quite late and as something of a Plan B.

The first airline in the world to introduce jet aircraft, the de Havilland Comet 1, was Great Britain's flag carrier BOAC, in May 1952. Aeroflot's first jet flight, with the Tu-104, took off in September 1956. Czech Airlines received their first Tu-104 in 1957. Pan Am's first jet service was a Boeing 707 from New York to Paris in October 1958, and Lufthansa received their first jet, also a Boeing 707, in 1960. JAT Yugoslav Airlines received their first Caravelle in 1963.

Compared to the world's big airlines, and even compared to some of their counterparts in the Warsaw Pact States, Interflug was lagging behind in its entry into the jet era. In 1967, the fleet stood at nine Il-18s, six An-24s, and the last four remaining Il-14s, which were about to leave the fleet. While Aeroflot was operating jets for more than a decade, Interflug was still waiting for their first example to arrive.

One of the reasons why Interflug only started flying jets so late was that the actual plan A had failed to materialise. In the late 1950s, maybe the most prestigious and ambitious industrial project in the entire country was the development of a GDR-built jet airliner, the Baade 152, which first flew in December 1958. Despite enormous effort and money invested, the Baade saw delay after delay, and then in March 1959, during only its second test flight, the prototype crashed. The project never recovered. Although a second prototype undertook another two test flights, delays and problems seemed to grow rather than shrink. When potential customer Aeroflot decided to opt for the Tu-104 instead of the Baade, the GDR government officially ended the project in 1961 because Interflug and the GDR's National People's Army were not sufficient to justify a production run.

With the Baade 152 project stopped, Interflug had to look elsewhere to satisfy their jet aircraft needs, and eventually chose the Tu-134 as the most suitable Plan B.

When the first jet was finally handed over to Interflug, the welcome it received by employees, company management and politicians was overwhelming. The sigh of relief, so it seemed, could be heard from Rostock to Dresden. This was a quantum leap for the airline, although it later turned out that the new type was not without problems and challenges.

The first two Tu-134s, DM-SCA and DM-SCB, was delivered to Schönefeld in October 1968, still flown by Russian pilots. Interflug's first in-house instructors started their training on the type in late summer 1968, just a few weeks before the delivery of the first aircraft. Back in the GDR, they were ready to pass on their knowledge to Interflug's line crews, most of whom transitioned from the An-24, quite a different aircraft compared to the Tu-134.

DM-SCA was the first Tu-134 to be delivered to Interflug in 1968
Previous image:
Tu-134 turnaround
Interflug Abteilung Werbung

Tu-134 DM-SCH seen at a wintry Poprad-Tatry Airport in Slovakia
Interflug Abteilung Werbung

Some nitpicking here: although the Tu-134s were the first jets operated by Interflug, they were not the first jets wearing Interflug colours. As early as the spring of 1965, the obscure and secretive Transport Squadron 44, the government flying unit, received a pair of Tu-124s, DM-SDA and DM-SDB, which were operated in 'camouflage' Interflug colours on government missions together, with a third ship wearing mostly white Air Force colours.

While Interflug's own crews were still getting trained, 'borrowed' Russian pilots started operating its first commercial Tu-134 flights. On December 5, 1968, Interflug's first commercial Tu-134 flight took off for Zagreb and Belgrade, followed by routes to Budapest, Sofia and Prague. At the same time, Interflug's future Tupolev cockpit crews were still doing training flights, getting ready to fully assume the operation of the new type. There were some challenges. First and foremost, the Tupolev was of course was much faster, which took some getting used to and for some pilots who previously mostly flew domestic routes on the An-24, talking to air traffic control in English was a new thing, too. The D-30 engines were not easy to handle, with much slower spool-up times compared to the prop-driven An-24 and Il-18 which responded immediately.

Passengers, on the other hand, soon grew to love the new jets. What is still true today was true in the late 1960s: for most passengers, a jet over a propeller is perceived as somehow more modern and 'better'. And that was true for the Tu-134. By summer 1969, an additional two more Tu-134s (DM-SCD and DM-SCH) were delivered to Interflug, bringing the fleet up to four. The operation was now entirely in Interflug's hands and the crews were up to speed on the type. Because the jets had a better image with passengers than the Il-18, whenever possible, the type was put on more prestigious international routes as well as the trips to the Black Sea (which saw a lot of travellers from West Berlin taking advantage of the cheap Interflug fares). Soon, the Tu-134 was operating many of Interflug's thinner but more prestigious European flights, and

The two noisiest, smokiest and most exhilerating airliners ever built meet in Leipzig in March 1986
Gottfried Schilke

even flew to the Middle East, taking over the service to Beirut and Damascus.

Compared to the Il-18, the Tupolev had 24 fewer seats (76 compared to 100) and its thirst for kerosene was significantly greater, so financially, the Tu-134 did not do much to improve Interflug's numbers. And operationally, the headaches remained. The Tu-134 needed more love by the maintenance crews than the sturdy Il-18, and Tu-134 flights were often cancelled and replaced by an Il-18. Interflug's top brass may not have minded too much as the Il-18's costs per seat were lower, but passenger reaction to the aircraft change, which sometimes happened at short notice, was less positive. When the Tupolevs did fly, both its crew of six (three in the cockpit and three in the cabin) and passengers liked the type.

In 1969, the GDR celebrated its 20th anniversary, and with a sufficient fleet and crew size, a dedicated Tu-134 squadron was founded. A special mission for the type in that year was flying the GDR's football team to Naples in Italy for a World Cup Qualifier. The Tu-134 also became a regular guest at Leipzig Airport, operating charter flights during the important Leipzig Trade Fair.

For a few years, the Tu-134 fleet remained at four aircraft, and only started to grow significantly when the improved Tupolev 134A version became available. The A variant was a bit longer than the basic version of the Tu-134 and improvements included upgraded engines with reverse thrust, and an auxiliary power unit (APU) to provide ground power. In February 1969, the first factory-new aircraft was picked up in Kharkiv by an Interflug crew not Russian pilots. More and more aircraft joined Interflug's fleet and the type found its mission operating the bulk of the airline's scheduled short and medium haul flights, including some routes to North Africa or the Middle East. Amsterdam, Copenhagen, Milan, Tirana, Damascus, Tunis were all Tupolev territory.

Charter flights were also occasionally flown by the 134, such as delivering the sailors of the GDR's fishing fleet to a ship (often in Scotland), sports teams to international events, or government and other delegations. Exceptional flights were rather seldom and mostly confined to flights within Europe (such as aid flights to Romania when an earthquake hit the country or flying workers to construction sites or fishing grounds around Europe). Compared to the often spectacular special missions the Il-18 operated, the life of the Tu-134 fleet was dull. One exception: in 1976, a dramatic mission took an Interflug Tu-134 to Afghanistan. A West German group of tourists suffered a bus accident close to the city of Jalalabad and quite interestingly and beyond all political conflicts, the (West) German Air Rescue requested Interflug's service and expertise to bring the tourists back home, a mission the airline completed with distinction.

There were major accidents involving the Tu-134 fleet. On September 1, 1975, DM-SCD crashed while on approach to Leipzig after a trade fair charter from Stuttgart, with the loss of 24 passengers (out of 28) and three crew (out of six). The flight was performing a precision approach radar (PAR) landing under the guidance of air traffic control. After descending below the minimum descent altitude (MDA), the left wing and left engine struck a radio mast. November 22, 1977 saw the second loss of a Tu-134 in Interflug service, in Schönefeld after a flight from Moscow. The approach was flown using the autopilot, which should have been disengaged before landing. After a heavy touchdown, one wing was torn off, the landing gear collapsed, and the fuselage quite spectacularly skidded along the runway for a few hundred meters. Looking at pictures of the remains of DM-SCM, it is surprising that none of the 81 passengers and crew died.

The Tu-134, although nowhere near perfect and with many operational compromises, became the workhorse in Interflug's fleet, taking care of most of the airline's short-haul flying. While the Il-62 took care of the longhaul network and the Il-18 found their role on busier shorthaul routes and the most exotic special missions, the Tu-134 performed yeoman service on Interflug's European network.

Over the years, Interflug operated three different versions. From outside,

Interflug Abteilung Werbung

they looked similar, but the cockpit design in particular came with huge differences, not making life easy for the flight deck crews, making them vulnerable to handling errors. The basic version was the Tu-134, with a glass nose for the navigator, no auxiliar power unit, a brake parachute, no reverse thrust, and the radar in a blister fairing under the nose. The Tu-134A version came with an auxiliary power unit (APU) as well as uprated Soloviev D-30 engines which had reverse thrust, dispensing with the braking parachute. Here, the navigator's office (the glass nose) was fully covered and the radar placed inside the cockpit. The navigator's station was now in the cockpit behind the pilots. The Tu-134AN version split the difference, coming with the glass nose and radar under the nose, but other than that had all the bells and whistles of the more modern 134A.

Interflug tried to standardize the cockpits of the three different variants as

A sharp portrait of DM-SCG, a Tupolev Tu-134K, enjoying some Italian sun at Milan Linate airport in July 1975
Jacques Barbé

Flight crew posing in front of a Tu-134
Interflug Abteilung Werbung

A classic view from the Schönefeld observation deck of a hardworking Tupolev between flights
Alan Bushell

much as they could to make the operation safer, but often met opposition from the manufacturer. Although it was possible to make smaller adjustments, the three versions retained their differences at least from a cockpit point of view.

Worth being mentioned are two Tu-134s which operated on behalf of the Stasi, DDR-SDI and DDR-SDH (wearing Interflug colours) as well as three Tu-134s operated by Transport Squadron 44 (TG-44), DDR-SDR, DDR-SDS and DDR-SDT. Two of them flew in (camouflage) Interflug colours, the third in the white GDR's Air Force design. The crews operating these very special missions were trained by Interflug and occasionally operated regular Interflug flights to accumulate the necessary flight hours and landings. As they wore regular Interflug uniforms during these missions, passengers would hardly have realised. All three, following the collapse of the GDR, were briefly registered in Croatia as 9A-ADL/P/R and wore "RPL Airports Rijeka" markings. Whatever that deal was, it fell through, and the three were briefly operated by the German Air Force as 11+10, 11+11 and 11+12 before being passed on to Russia eventually, where they all flew with Aeroflot.

Interflug's Tu-134s fleet reached its peak at 23 ships in the early 1980s. Some were delivered fresh from the factory, others inherited from the National People's Army after already flying there for a couple of years. Receiving used aircraft from the military was not really popular but as so often, the decision was not with Interflug's management, but taken on a higher level.

During the early days of commercial flying, the aircraft produced in the Soviet Union were on a comparable technological level to their counterparts in the west, e.g. the Il-62 vs. the VC10, or the Tupolev

Pushback time at Schönefeld
Interflug Abteilung Werbung

134 vs. early DC9s or Caravelles. But as time advanced, more modern aircraft like the newer versions of the Boeing 737 and the first Airbus A320s appeared, and the technological distance between Western and Eastern aircraft types began to widen. Even new developments like the Tu-154M or the Ilyushin Il-86 (which went into service in late 1980, nearly a decade after the first Airbus A300 took off, and only two years behind the Boeing 767) had huge deficiencies and were not able to compete. Even though efficient aircraft were on the market, Eastern Bloc airlines like Interflug were not able to buy from the West, at least not for the time being. Despite knowing that its fleet of Il-62s, Tu-134s and Il-18s was not state-of-the-art, management had little choice but to continue with what they had.

Another increasing problem was noise regulations were getting ever stricter at most European airports, usually in the form of punishing landing fees for noisier birds. The Tu-134 was among the noisiest commercial jets and not really welcome at many airports any longer.

At the point Interflug stopped flying in 1991, some 19 Tu-134s were still listed in the fleet, and it was a Tu-134, D-AOBC, that had the ambiguous honour to operate the last-ever Interflug commercial flight, on April 30, 1991, from Vienna to Schönefeld, effectively closing the airline down with its landing. The welcome after its landing was, as one can imagine, much less euphoric and festive than 23 years earlier, when the first Interflug Tu-134 touched down in Schönefeld. In those 23 years, the little Tupolev had become an indispensable part of Interflug's operation right up until the end of the airline. After the fall of the Iron Curtain, most other European airlines operating the type (Malév, LOT, Balkan et al) were quite quick to replace theirs fleets with more efficient and quieter aircraft, and Interflug had such plans, too. The difference was that they didn't materialise before the end of the airline.

Fortunately, a number of Tu-134s still survive in Germany to this day, some in really good condition, and most wearing Interflug colours: DDR-SCB is stored at the airport of Magdeburg in rather good condition. Sister ship DDR-SCH is conserved in the aviation museum in Finowfurt, northeast of Berlin. After being painted in hybrid Interflug / LOT colours for the shooting of a movie, it was repainted in full Interflug colours. DDR-SCK is in excellent condition, wears full Interflug colours once more, and is part of the fantastic exhibition of the Flugausstellung Hermeskeil, where Il-18 DDR-STH is also on display. DDR-SCZ is on display at the Flugzeug- und Technikmuseum in Merseburg, close to Leipzig. It appears to be in quite good condition but is definitely in need of a proper cleanup or repaint. Another Tu-134 survivor is DDR-SCL, bought by Hydro Systems, a supplier for the aviation industry based in the city of Biberach in the Black Forest. On January 29, 1990, the aircraft was flown to the former Canadian military base of Lahr (with an intermediate stop in Stuttgart), from where it was taken to Biberach by road. The aircraft wears the blue and white Hydro company colours. Even though no longer wearing Interflug colours, it is at least another survivor of the airlines's Tu-134 fleet. Alas one bird that didn't escape the scrapper was DDR-SCF. Parked at Leipzig Airport for many years (and in increasingly sad condition), the aircraft was eventually scrapped in summer 2013 (unlike Interflug's first Il-18, DM-STA, which was repainted in the beautiful blue and white Deutsche Lufthansa colours and is now on display in front of the terminal there). All the ex-Interflug Tu-134s that saw commercial service with another airline went to Russia initially. Most remained there, flying for airlines like Tyumenaviatrans, Komiinteravia (later UTair or UTair Express), or Sibaviatrans (which became part of the Air Union group). Some went on to Kazakhstan, and one unfortunate example, formerly DDR-SCT, ended its life in a crash in Nigeria while it was leased out to Harco Air Services. While some of them seem to remain in storage (ex DDR-SDU is still parked at the airport of Arkhangelsk in Northern Russia, looking stunning in full Aeroflot colours), none remain in service.

Interflug Abteilung Werbung

The Ilyushin Il-62: the flagship

The Ilyushin Il-62, more than any other type it ever operated, catapulted Interflug into a new league, especially due to its 5,000 mile (8,000 kilometre) range, which created new long haul opportunities for the airline – Asia, the Americas, southern Africa. In some cases these ports were previously served, but with multiple stops or higher fuel burn en route.

It also offered unprecedented comfort for passengers used to the noisy (and much slower) Ilyushin Il-18 which operated most of Interflug's longest trips prior to the introduction of the Il-62. And it arrived at the perfect time: in the early 1970s, the two Germanys formally recognised each other, stepping back from a hostile stance to a more pragmatic relationship. Recognition by West Germany paved the way for improved international relations for the GDR, with many new embassies opening abroad, and growing demand for travel (albeit a large portion of the GDR's citizens were excluded).

April 22, 1970 was a big day for Interflug and its employees: the first Il-62, DM-SEA, was delivered to Berlin Schönefeld from the factory in Kazan. The airline had only entered the jet age less than two years prior when its first Tupolev Tu-134 went into service in July 1968. Interflug's proud employees were delighted to have finally caught up to some of its fellow airlines not only from the West but also in fraternal Warsaw Pact countries. While the Tupolev was a speedy little jet that fulfilled its short- and medium haul role reasonably well, it did not get close to the glamour and prestige that came with the introduction of a big long-haul jet like the Il-62.

Most of the early pilots trained on the new flagship previously flew the Il-18 and thus had the necessary long-haul experience, while others followed from the Tu-134 pilot pool. Only a few weeks after the first Il-62 got delivered, a second ship, DM-SEB, touched down in Schönefeld on June 2, 1970. And, hard to imagine in today's efficient world, the first scheduled Il-62 flight was not operated until almost two months later: to Sofia on July 28, 1970. A few days later, it operated on the prestigious and ever-busy Moscow route, followed by a longer haul, to Baghdad via Damascus.

The Il-62 made Interflug more competitive. On the Moscow route, Aeroflot had been offering jet service for a decade with their Tupolev Tu-104, followed by the Tu-134 and their own Il-62, and became passengers' preferred choice. With the Il-62, Interflug was able to offer not only a similar but an even better experience to travellers and catch up with Aeroflot.

But even though the type was more capable than the Il-18, the Il-62, at least before the upgrade to M standard, had its shortcomings, most notably with the Kuznetsov NK-8 engines on the basic version which were noisy, inefficient and left the aircraft underpowered, especially on a hot day out of Baghdad where summer temperatures could reach 50C (122F). When the Il-62M version became available, powered by Soloviev D-30 turbofans, fuel savings of 15 percent were achieved, with more efficient thrust reversers, less fuel burn and less noise. Other modifications that came with the M included an extra fuel tank installed in the vertical fin able to take an additional 5,000 litres of kerosene, giving the aircraft both more payload and range, upgraded avionics in the cockpit, and evolved passenger cabin architecture.

Over the years, Interflug operated six original non-M Il-62s, and twelve Il-62Ms. When it started flying for Interflug, the Il-62 soon took most of the airline's long-haul flights and, in between intercontinental trips, was also sequenced on busy European flights such as the 'Friendship Line' to Moscow and its main link to Western Europe, Amsterdam (which, given that the airline wasn't permitted to fly over West Germany, took over two hours, tracking due north overhead the Baltic Sea and Denmark before turning south over the North Sea into Schiphol airport).

Not only offering more range than any other type in Interflug's fleet, but with 168 seats, significantly more capacity, so putting it on the busiest routes in the network made a lot of sense. By 1973, including the loss of DM-SEA in August 1972, the Il-62 fleet had grown to five aircraft (in spring 1973, three ships were delivered from Kazan in just three weeks).

The first upgraded Il-62M delivered to Interflug was DM-SEI, joining the fleet in October 1980. But even though more and more of the advanced M version were delivered, the classic non-M Kuznetsov Il-62s all remained in service with Interflug until the late 1980s. The youngest, DDR-SEH, was not retired until November 1989.

Travelling on the Il-62 got you the highest level of comfort on any of Interflug's Soviet-built aircraft, and the aircraft was popular with passengers and crews alike. Its enormous wing meant the ship remained very stable even in turbulent weather, and with the four engines mounted on the rear of the fuselage, was very quiet inside the cabin, unlike the very noisy Il-18.

As well as its role as the airline flagship, it was also used for government

Leipzig, 1986
Gottfried Schilke
Previous image: Spectacular Il-62 takeoff
Peter Zimmermann via Bundesarchiv

DDR-SEM taken from Schönefeld's observation deck in 1990 only months before it was sold to Aeroflot
Gottfried Schilke

missions (to be fair, it wasn't always easy to tell where scheduled flying stopped and government missions started). In November 1974, following a series of charter flights (most of them carrying crews of the GDR's fishing fleets), a scheduled route to Havana was launched, designated IF900/901. Once more, the capabilities of the Il-62 had opened a new door for the GDR on the world stage.

To be able to cross the Atlantic Ocean, three machines, DM-SEF, DM-SEG and DM-SHE, were equipped with the expensive LORAN-B radio navigation system. Even though it had more range than the other aircraft in Interflug's fleet, strong westerly winds made non-stop westbound flights to Cuba impossible with a full payload. For the first year of operations, a technical stop for refuelling was made Santa Maria in the Azores, a stop that Cubana had also chosen for the same route.

In March 1976, the stop was moved from the Azores to Gander in Newfoundland, Canada. Operating via Gander saved more than 400 miles (645 kilometres) off the Azores route. Sometimes, when the wind conditions were favourable and or the payload lighter than usual, the return flight was operated non-stop. The stop in Canada was not very popular with the GDR regime – dissidents occasionally used it as a means of defecting to the West. Instead of returning to the aircraft from the transit lounge, they prostrated themselves before a Canadian immigration officer and applied for political asylum.

The story goes that sometimes, the most pragmatic planned their escape for the return flight from Cuba to the GDR. Why not enjoy a holiday in tropical Cuba before saying goodbye to the system? Imagine their horror at the captain's welcome-aboard announcement leaving Havana that due to favourable winds, the flight would be operating nonstop back to Berlin.

What was known as the Gander Gap was only overcome with the delivery of the Airbus A310s, which were able to fly the route to Havana non-stop in both directions. But then, a few months later, the GDR was gone anyway.

In the late 1980s, the Il-62 was used for a major expansion; between 1985 and 1989, Interflug took over nine additional aircraft including two inherited from the GDR Air Force's TG-44 government flying squadron. New routes were opened to Dubai, Beijing and Singapore, followed by Malta, Bangkok and Mexico City, part of a new strategy to serve major

Those Soloviev D-30s keep on turning
Previous page: The tech ops dream team: Russian hardware, German maintenance

Interflug Abteilung Werbung

hub airports in the respective regions, allowing passengers to connect within the region from there, and in the case of some routes, blatantly catering to demand from West Germany, which brought in much-needed hard currency.

Less commercially attractive routes, which were often flown because of political rather than commercial reasons, were dropped, such as Maputo, Amman and Baghdad. The 1989 summer schedule shows the Il-62 deployed on a cosmopolitan mix of destinations, some only an hour's flying time from base, others taking days to complete: Amsterdam, Athens, Beijing, Bourgas, Brazzaville, Bucharest, Budapest, Cairo, Damascus, Dubai, Hanoi, Havana, Helsinki, Istanbul, Karachi, Larnaca, Leningrad, Luanda, Malta, Moscow, Rome, Singapore, Tripoli, Tunis and Varna. This demonstrated the Il-62's diverse capabilities.

Right up until the end of Interflug, the Il-62 fulfilled an essential role, and even when the A310s replaced it on many of the long-haul flights, it still had a place as a high-capacity people mover on shorter flights, and as a supplement aircraft, as the fleet had quite a bit of spare capacity. When Interflug launched the route from Leipzig to Düsseldorf in August 1989, Il-62 DDR-SET had the honour of operating the inaugural flight (which still routed via Czechoslovakian airspace, as crossing the intra-German border was still forbidden to German airlines).

When Interflug stopped flying, the active Il-62 fleet stood at seven ships. All seven were sold to what was still the Uzbek division of Aeroflot, based at Tashkent (a major aerospace service centre for Soviet-built types), which became Uzbekistan Airways in 1992. Except for two, all of them were broken up or remain in storage in Tashkent. DDR-SEY suffered a fatal landing accident at Mashhad while operating for Iranian carrier Aria Airlines (leased from Deta Air of Kazakhstan) in July 2009. One of the very last active Il-62s in the world is an ex Interflug machine, and not even their youngest one. DDR-SET was delivered new to Berlin in December 1985, converted to a freighter after its Uzbek days, and is still operating today for Rada Airlines of Belarus as EW-450TR.

Whether a sign of Interflug's enthusiasm for the type or poor fleet planning ability, their last two Il-62s,

The only regular Western European port of call for the Il-62 was Amsterdam
Interflug Abteilung Werbung

DDR-SEY and DDR-SEZ, were only delivered to Interflug in June and August 1989, at the same time the three A310s were handed over. So Interflug took delivery of more of old iron and its replacement at exactly the same time.

Unfortunately, even though it was an overall success for Interflug, the Il-62 also had the sad honour of being the type with the highest number of fatalities in accidents. Interflug lost two Il-62s including its first delivered, DM-SEA, in what is still Germany's worst ever air disaster, hardly more than two years after its handover, with just 3,500 hours of flight in the log book. On the late afternoon of August 14, 1972, just minutes after takeoff from Schönefeld on a non-scheduled charter flight bound for the Bulgarian seaside resort Bourgas, leaking hot air ducts in the air conditioning system caused a fire to erupt in the rear of the aircraft. With no fire detection sensors that far aft, the first sign of trouble was unresponsive elevator control. Despite turning back, control was lost and the aircraft crashed close to the town of Königs Wusterhausen, killing all 156 people onboard.

The other Il-62 loss occurred 17 years later, on June 17, 1989. While taxiing out at the start of the sunrise IF102 departure to Moscow, the flight deck crew omitted to deactivate gust locks that held control surfaces in place during parking. Although 'full and free' controls appeared twice on the checklist, control surfaces were still locked; at 160 knots (300 kilometres per hour), the captain could not get the nose up and called for an abort, with just 940 metres (3,080 feet) remaining of runway two five left. The flight engineer panicked and instead of putting the engines into reverse thrust, accidentally shut down all four engines. DDR-SEW went off the end of the runway at 141 knots (262 kilometres per hour) and smashed through lighting stanchions, an excavation ditch, a water tank, a road embankment, the

Tino Lehmann

Interflug Abteilung Werbung

concrete piles of the airport perimeter fence, and six large trees. Testament to the strength of the Il-62, only 21 people lives were lost, with 92 survivors (including all ten crew). It is possible that even more lives could have been saved, but rescue operations were delayed as authorities feared sabotage – as the crash took place on the anniversary of the 1953 anti-Soviet uprising and against a backdrop of palpable political tension of the GDR's last months.

These two tragic events should not cast a shadow over an otherwise quite remarkable legacy. And to finish this chapter on a positive note: Interflug's Il-62s were famous throughout the GDR thanks to a high profile television career as the secret star of the Treffpunkt Flughafen television drama series first broadcast in 1985 and 1986.

The Tupolev Tu-154: why Interflug never flew them

Aeroflot had hundreds of them, and the type was the backbone of the fleet of CSA, Malév, Balkan, LOT, Cubana, and post-revolutionary Iran: the Tupolev Tu-154. The only airline from the Warsaw Pact countries to never operate the type commercially was Interflug.

As the type was a very versatile medium-haul aircraft, popular with passengers and airlines alike, this is quite surprising. When the first variants of the Tu-154 appeared on the market in the early 1970s, Interflug already had the Tu-134 and Ilyushin Il-62 in operation. With East Germany being in the centre of Europe, the Tu-134 was able to cover all European destinations and even reach cities in the Middle East. The Il-62 (together with the Il-18 propliners) did all the longhaul flying to destinations in Asia, Africa and the Americas. It was much more capable in terms of range than any of the early variants of the Tu-154 and could lift a greater payload.

In order to add another aircraft type to the fleet, the Tu-154's commercial and/or operational advantages would have had to be fantastic. So while there is very little to be found in the archive of actual plans to add the type to the fleet, it is safe to assume that the Tu-154 was under consideration, and more than once. Its role would have been as a replacement for the ageing fleet of Il-18s, in between the Tu-134 and Il-62 both in terms of range and the number of passengers.

But, and that is probably the main reason why the type never entered service with Interflug: the technical details and specifications promised on paper were not met by the type's early variants in reality, making it an unattractive proposition when the Interflug fleet was already capable of handling all the missions of the airline.

Thus, fleet planners came to the conclusion that adding Il-62s to its existing fleet and keeping the Il-18 in the air a bit longer than planned was indeed the better choice for the airline, better than adding another type would add complexity to the fleet without much benefit, and might not even deliver on the performance promised by the Tupolev Design Bureau.

A second chance for the trijet came with the more capable Tu-154M in the early 1980s, but by then, more modern types like the Tu-204 were already on the horizon. A quite popular official Interflug poster bearing the title "Kurs 2000", which translates approximately as "Heading 2000", displays the Tu-204 and Il-96 as future types (still available to buy as a nostalgic metal sign for bars and man caves). Thus the type was dismissed by Interflug for a second time.

By the time the Tu-204 and Il-96 were ready for primetime, Interflug was

One of two GDR government Tu-154s disguised as civilian airliners, Schönefeld, 1990   Ralf Manteufel
Previous image: Tu-154M cockpit in flight   Simon De Rudder

looking for Boeing 737s (and timetables were published showing the type); the Fokker 100 or BAe146 were also possible candidates.

But then, if Interflug never operated the type, why did at least two Tu-154s (DDR-SFA and DDR-SFB) wear Interflug colours? These two Tu-154Ms were operated by the Transportfliegergeschwader 44 (TG-44), a squadron of the Air Force of the National People's Army. The primary task of the squadron was the transport of the political leadership of the German Democratic Republic by aeroplanes and helicopters. Since the borders between Interflug and the Air Forces Of The National People's Army were often a bit blurry, and also in order to conceal their sometimes sensitive missions, many of the squadron's aircraft wore Interflug painting.

Most of them were based at the super-secret airport of Marxwalde (today Neuhardenberg), east of Berlin, and would only appear at Schönefeld Airport occasionally. Thus, if you saw a Tu-154 wearing Interflug colours at an airport somewhere outside the GDR, it was likely on a government mission, carrying high-ranking politicians or officials on an official (or not so official) visit.

Both Tu-154s (at least a third aircraft was supposed to enter service with the Air Force also) were passed on to the all-German Air Force, or Luftwaffe, after the reunification of both countries. They were registered 11+01 and 11+02 and for a short period, both were used on shuttle flights, bringing government officials and politicians between the old German capital Bonn to the new capital Berlin.

In 1993, conversion of the aircraft into reconnaissance aircraft began. Special optical cameras and electronic sensors were installed for the CSCE (Conference for Security and

Cooperation in Europe) and its "Open Skies Missions". Unfortunately, no Traffic Alert and Collision Avoidance System (TCAS) was installed during this upgrade, which most likely could have avoided a tragic accident.

On September 13, 1997, over the lonely South Atlantic Ocean, 11+02 collided with a US Air Force C-141 in mid-air, killing all onboard both aircraft. The German jet was flying from Cologne to Cape Town with a fuel stop in Niamey, Niger. On the second leg, its flight plan was not forwarded to controllers at Windhoek Centre in Namibia, who were unaware of the German jet. Since both aircraft went missing at the same time, a midair collision was suspected, and three days after the crash, the first pieces of wreckage were found in the ocean, and after six days, the first body, German flight attendant Saskia Neumeyer.

The Luftwaffe acknowledged that their crew were mostly at fault, as they were flying in breach of the so-called Semicircular Rule, whereby a cruising altitude (especially in un- or poorly-controlled airspace) is selected based on the direction of flight, to reduce the odds of a head-on collision, which is that above 29,000 feet, aircraft flying on a heading of 000 to 179 degrees (essentially, eastbound) will cruise at FL290, FL330, FL370; and on headings of 180 to 359 degrees (westbound), the ship will cruise at FL310, FL350, FL390.

Upon this accident, sister ship 11+01 was retired from service with the Luftwaffe, briefly flew in Russia as RA-85092 and was later sold to Iran, where it flew with Iran Air Tours and later Eram Air and was apparently retired from service in 2009, ending the story of the GDR's Tu-154s two decades after the end of the GDR.

Interflug TU-154M DDR-SFA taking off　　　　　　　　　　　Luftfahrtarchiv Matthias Winkler

Interflug colours as camouflage: the aircraft of TG-44 and Stasi

In the previous chapter we discussed the non-career of the Tupolev Tu-154 with Interflug, and why there were still two Tu-154s seen flying in Interflug colours. They are just one example of aircraft that were painted in Interflug colours but did not actually fly for the airline. Two government branches flying aircraft in Interflug livery were the mysterious Transportfliegergeschwader 44 and the other was the Ministry of State Security (often simply refered to as the Stasi).

Transportfliegergeschwader (Transport Flying Squadron) 44 was founded by ministerial order in July 1957 (it was initially known as the Regierungsfliegerstaffel, or Government Flying Squadron). The squadron's primary task was transporting members of the government and other VIPs with a mixed fleet of aircraft and helicopters. The squadron's first aircraft was a salon-equipped piston-driven Ilyushin Il-14 registered DM-SBM, delivered in July 1957.

The airfield close to the town of Marxwalde was chosen as the squadron's headquarters, around 70 kilometers (just under 45 miles) east of Berlin and quite close to the Polish border. This remote and well-hidden field had already served as a secret airport during the 1930s, so it was a return to an old role after a very quiet twelve years between 1945 and 1957.

In order to accomodate the new squadron, its staff and aircraft, some infrastructure upgrades became necessary, all under the cover of secrecy. The squadron at its new headquarters officially opened in March 1959, when helicopters and aircraft were moved to Marxwalde from two smaller airfields in Niederlehme and Strausberg as well as Schönefeld Airport, from where the Il-14s mostly flew.

A driving force behind its creation was the country's leader (officially General Secretary of the Socialist Unity Party) Walter Ulbricht. Ulbricht was very ambitious and one of his interests was aviation and in particular creating a competitive aerospace sector in the GDR. The locally-built Baade 152 did fly and went on a few test flights but was abandoned after a crash, and it crucially lacked the support of the Soviet Union. Apart from building up the GDR's own aviation industry, Ulbricht was also very much after a flag carrier to be proud of, and creating state-of-the-art transportation for himself and his government, which also brought with it some much-needed status symbols, which would have included Baade 152s not only to be the flagship of Interflug but to put his country in the tiny club of nations with a locally-built jet-powered Air Force One.

Throughout the GDR's existence, one of the ambitions of its government was to stand next to its bigger German neighbour and experience the same level of recognition and respect. And sometimes, even small events left a lasting impression: in the late 1950s, Walter Ulbricht travelled to Moscow for a state visit onboard his Il-14. He was absolutely not happy to see that West German chancellor Konrad Adenauer took the same trip just a few days earlier with a much more impressive Lockheed Super Constellation. Only one year later, the squadron began replacing its Il-14s with bigger and more capable turbine-powered four-engined Il-18s.

TG-44 joined the jet age with a trio of Tu-124s. DM-SDA wore full regular Interflug colours. Sister ship DM-SDB had a slightly abridged version of the Interflug colours with a more elaborated cheatline. The third ship was only registered with the military "495" designation and only wore Air Force colours. During the ten years they operated for the squadron, their career wasn't necessarily much shorter than that of other types, but they were not transferred to Interflug for secondary use, instead going to the USSR, with one frame still extant today: DM-SDB has recently been refurbished, painted in Aeroflot colours and put on display in a park in the Russian city of Kimry, where constructor Andrey Tupolev was born.

Everything in Marxwalde was top secret and the squadron's existence was entwinded with rumours and legends until its end, because people working there had to keep their mouth shut and everybody else could fill in the gaps with guesswork and supposition. Following several re-organizations and name changes, the unit finally got its name TG-44 in 1973 and was later christened the 'Arthur Pieck squadron' after the first general director of Interflug. This name choice illustrates, among other things, the blurring of the lines between the civilian airline of the GDR and its military branches. More than often, the separation was quite diffuse and it was not always easy to tell where the airline ended and the military began.

Of all the units that were part of the GDR's National People's Army, TG-44 was easily among the most elitist and also most mysterious. After all, hardly anybody experienced more proximity to the leadership of the country. Thus becoming part of the TG-44 squadron was a great honour and privilege, but it came with a few downsides, too. Members were not allowed to talk about their missions, take notes or document them in any way, not even to close relatives. That is also why few pictures exist of its aircraft or infrastructure. Being discrete went with the territory of being in such a privileged group.

The upside wasn't only prestige, it was also international travel. Throughout the GDR's existence, travelling remained the exclusive preserve of only a fortunate few, so the squadron was lucky as its personnel were able to leave the country quite frequently. The selection process for anybody working here was very strict and included neverending background and loyalty checks, even more than for civilian Interflug crew. Members of the TG-44 were representatives of the country and expected to be über-loyal.

Throughout its existence, the GDR was obsessed with people leaving the country. So in reality, while they did leave the country on official missions, squadron members were quite restricted when it came to discovering the world during their trips abroad; for instance, no crew member was supposed to leave the hotel and walk around the city by themselves.

The Tupolev nobody wanted to fly on, the Stasi's Tu-134 DDR-SDI during a brief visit to Nice Airport
Previous image: Tu-134 DDR-SDI hiding behind a palm tree at Nice Airport
Alan Bushell

This TG-44 bird started out as DDR-SDU in disguise as an Interflug bird, became 11+12 in the unified German Air Force, briefly registered in Croatia as 9A-ADR with RPL Airports Rijeka titles, and ended its days with Aeroflot Nord
Sebastian Schmitz

This National People's Army machine carried the military registration 184
Luftfahrtarchiv Matthias Winkler

The same ship, after serving in the united German Air Force as 11+11, in brief storage Croatia as 9A-ADL, awaiting the next chapter of its career as RA-65566 with Aeroflot
Sebastian Schmitz

Tupolev Tu-124 DM-SDB at Dubrovnik Airport in 1965
Jacques Guillem collection

Even though they were carefully scrutinised, there was always the risk of a defection during a layover. Crewmembers were expected to 'take good care' of each other – in other words, supervise the rest of the team. And as if that wasn't enough, members of the Stasi were onboard most flights as well. On some trips, crew would also occasionally meet West Germans abroad. In that case, making any form of contact was even less desirable. More prosaically, government trips have tightly-timed itineraries. So, in many cases, crews often didn't see more of a foreign country than the airport and a hotel room.

Another disadvantage for the squadron's crews was that they were more or less on permanent duty, as a sudden government flight could be scheduled at any time of the day or night, and often at very short notice. For family or private life or maintaining a social network, they paid a hefty price by being on permanent standby.

Before a government visit, there was often a rehearsal flight where a crew flew the actual itinerary and checked everything on the ground at the different airports that would be visited to be prepared for all eventualities. Such trips preceding the actual state visits or official missions also added flight hours and time away from their homebase for aircraft and crews. During its peak, TG-44 had more than 1,000 staff taking care of its aircraft and flying them. Most lived in Marxwalde right next to the airfield in a very rural part of the GDR and quite a sharp contrast to their trips abroad.

While helicopters of the squadron (the main type over the years was the Mil Mi-8) wore military camouflage, things were a bit different with the squadron's bigger aircraft types, as these increasingly travelled abroad. Starting in the 1960s, after initially being painted in the quite nondescript colours of the GDR Air Force, the squadron's larger aircraft were painted in Interflug colours and the crews flying them, although they were soldiers, started wearing Interflug uniforms on many of their missions.

Overflight rights were one of the reasons for doing so. In the GDR's early days, not many countries recognised the GDR and international relations often ranged from difficult to hostile. With aircraft painted in a regular airline's paint scheme and crews wearing Interflug uniforms instead of military attire, things usually got a lot easier, as a civilian flight will be granted overflight rights more generously than a government flight, especially that of an unrecognised or hostile country.

Another reason the aircraft wore Interflug paint was keeping their official (and sometimes delicate) missions under cover. The average citizen was not able to tell the difference between a regular Interflug aircraft or one operated by TG-44 or Stasi, in particular as the types were largely the same ones that the airline operated (An-24, Tu-134 or Il-62). Two exceptions, where the type was not operated by Interflug, were the Tu-124, which TG-44 operated three of between 1965 and 1975, and the two Tu-154s which joined the squadron only in 1989.

Top politicians, like most VIPs, had their peculiarities. Walter Ulbricht was known by the crews to be obsessed with the cabin temperature. He insisted on a temperature of 25° C (77F) in the cabin and checked the thermostat on the cabin wall first thing when he boarded the plane. Crews knew of this fad and before he boarded, they made sure that the thermostat showed 25°C, knowing that he would be happy.

Erich Honecker was known to often show up in the cockpit during longer flights, sometimes in the middle of the night in his pyjamas, to find out about the progress of the flight. Other government members were known to spend whole flights lasting many hours playing cards. Nobody got to know the leadership as intimately as the members of TG-44.

In order to understand the development of the squadron over the years, it is helpful to understand the political developments at the time, as they largely went hand in hand. The political situation in the early days of the GDR was such that there was not a lot of long-haul flying to do for its government fleet, as the GDR was only recognised by socialist countries of the Warsaw Pact and some allies; and rival West Germany was very keen on keeping things that way. Their so-called Hallstein doctrine was a policy which stated that the Federal Republic would not establish or maintain diplomatic relations with any country recognising the GDR. West Germany's point of view was that there was only one Germany, and furthermore, that the right to represent it fell to the West German government. With West Germany already quite strong politically and economically at the time the doctrine was implemented in 1955, many countries felt under pressure not to establish (at least official) relations with the GDR. A similar situation to that of China and Taiwan today! The GDR's successive governments always tried to make their nation 'part of the club' to bestow legitimacy. (Indeed one of Erich Honecker's greatest foreign policy achievement was getting the GDR admitted to the United Nations as a full member in September 1973, which helped normalise the existence of the country with the rest of the world.)

It was the GDR's belief that the more countries would recognise the GDR, the safer and more irrevocable its long-term existence and the division of Germany, as well as internally cement the position of the governing Socialist Unity Party. In early 1965, GDR foreign diplomacy saw a small breakthrough: Walter Ulbricht was invited for an official state visit to Egypt. West Germany was not happy and lobbied hard against the trip. An Il-18 took off but only got as far as Dubrovnik (then in Yugoslavia). From there, Ulbricht had to make the rest of his journey by cruise ship, as German NATO ally Greece would not grant overflight rights to his plane. While he did not land in Cairo as planned, Ulbricht received a quite triumphant welcome in the port of Alexandria and West Germany suffered a diplomatic defeat.

In 1970, following a power struggle for the top job, Erich Honecker first became First Secretary of the Central Committee and chairman of the National Defence Council. What sounds so awkward effectively meant: the boss of the country, and head of state. Under Honecker's helm, foreign politics changed quite significantly and the GDR opened up a bit more to the world.

And the same happened across the border, as West Germany realised that its unyielding strategy towards the GDR did not result in much. From now on, a more pragmatic course was chosen. Negotiations between both countries took place and delegations travelled back and forth between both countries. In 1972, both Germanys signed the so-called Basic Treaty, a document concerning the relation of both countries. For the first time, they recognised each other, which opened the door to membership in the United Nations as members 133 and 134, as well as a much wider level of recognition internationally.

For GDR politicians and diplomats alike, a new era began and this meant new opportunities to travel abroad. There was a lot of catching up to do as more and more countries recognised the smaller of the two Germanys, and state visits by Erich Honecker to all parts of the world followed suit. By the end of the 1970s, the GDR had commenced diplomatic relationships with most countries in the world, with embassies, trade or military missions were opened, and these needed to be staffed and supplied – another responsibility which fell to TG-44.

The squadron's fleet reflected the increased amount and longer distances of government travel. By 1975, all Tu-124s were transferred to the Soviet Union, and at the same time, the Il-18s were transferred to Interflug (with decades of commercial life ahead of them). Both were largely replaced by incoming Tu-134s, with up to 11 on strength.

TG-44 not only flew official government missions. Whatever was in the interest of the country could become a flight assignment: projecting power or economic interests by sending scientists, business delegations, engineers or diplomats around the globe was the squadron's everyday business. Solidarity with allied or befriended countries also played a big role and the squadron's aircraft were quite frequently used for 'solidarity flights' to countries like Ethiopia, Vietnam, Mozambique, Afghanistan, North Korea and Nicaragua. Occasionally, foreign heads of state or politicians that enjoyed the support of the GDR government used the squadron's aircraft for their own international travels, including Nicaragua's Daniel Ortega and Palestine's Yassir Arafat. Occasionally, some of the squadron's aircraft also helped out on Interflug flights when there was a shortage, such as after the crash of Interflug's flagship Il-62 DM-SEA in August 1972.

With the mission expanding, TG-44's fleet requirements changed and sometimes aircraft were stretched to the limit of their capabilities, such as sending a short haul Tu-134 to Mozambique, not really the perfect aircraft for such missions. But help was on the way: in 1978, the first of what would eventually become five different Il-62s joined the squadron, delivered to Schönefeld fresh from the factory in Kazan, registered DM-SEK in full Interflug colours. With the Il-62, the GDR finally had a world class head of state transport, able to stand proud on the tarmac at any summit of world leaders.

Like all the other government aircraft, it was part of the squadron based in Marxwalde but the 2,400 metre (7,874 foot) runway was too small to handle such large aircraft on a regular basis. And as most government flights originated in the capital city anyway, the Il-62s were based at Schönefeld Airport.

Painted in full Interflug colours, they operated exclusively on government missions. Even though the details were a matter of secrecy, everybody at Schönefeld knew they were not part of the regular Interflug fleet. When the GDR's registration changed back from DM- to DDR- in 1981, DM-SEK became DDR-SEK. In 1979, a second Il-62 joined the squadron, DDR-SEL, and in 1982, Il-62 number three, DDR-SEN was delivered via Tashkent. In 1984 and 1987, the oldest two Il-62s were handed down to Interflug to continue flying commercially, something that happened routinely when GDR government aircraft reached a certain age or number of hours. DDR-SEK and -SEL were replaced by two brand new Il-62s, DDR-SEP and DDR-SEV in 1984 and 1987, and these two served with the squadron until the end of the GDR alongside DDR-SEN.

In 1983, a snapshot of the squadron's fleet saw eleven Tu-134s, three Il-62s, and six Mi-8 helicopters. A pair of Tu-154Ms, DDR-SFA and -SFB were delivered in 1988, with plans calling for a third ship but these never materialised.

Il-62 11+20 on the day of the German reunification, October 3, 1990, just having been reregistered
Luftfahrtarchiv Matthias Winkler

While the late 1970s and early 1980s were good years for the GDR as far as international relations were concerned, its population did not see any great progress or improvement in their material quality of life or personal freedom, leading to a great deal of frustration on the part of the populace. The government tried to team up with other countries, looking for investment or business opportunities to jumpstart the economy.

Honecker was a very frequent flyer at the time, traveling to Asia, the Americas, and officially met with both US president Gerald Ford and West German chancellor Helmut Schmidt. He even visited Pope John Paul II in the Vatican. His biggest dream, however, was a proper state visit to West Germany. But there, the Soviet Union, which always had a strong say in GDR foreign diplomacy, had strong reservations. It was only in 1987, that Michail Gorbachev said "Da," and Erich Honecker went on his state visit to Bonn, the capital of West Germany, and to Munich, on a five-day state visit. Landing in Cologne aboard Il-62 DDR-SEP and greeted on the tarmac by his West-German counterpart chancellor Helmut Kohl was probably Erich's greatest moment. With international relations becoming a lot more relaxed and the GDR recognised by most countries in the world, painting its government aircraft into Interflug colours was less of a necessity, but this habit never changed until the end of the country.

The Stasi had its own fleet, and like TG-44, also wore Interflug colours but did not actually operate for the airline. From 1967 to 1977, An-24 DM-SBH flew for the Stasi's Fluggruppe 10 (Flying Group 10) in full Interflug colours until it was replaced by a pair of Tu-134s, DDR-SDH and DDR-SDI. These aircraft were much less active than those belonging to TG-44 and mostly based out of Schönefeld Airport where they were operated and maintained by Interflug staff but exclusively used by the Ministry, a bit like a wet lease.

Their busiest period was probably just before the Berlin wall came down, a final rebellion by the increasingly insecure state institutions trying to plug ever-growing leaks in the façade of normality. The urge for many GDR citizens to leave the country was growing stronger by the day, via either illegal routes, or, as became possible with growing liberalisation in other Warsaw Pact nations, via the borders that Hungary or Poland shared with the West. The Stasi planes were used for repatriation flights of GDR citizens back home from abroad and it is safe to assume that these aircraft saw a lot of unhappy passengers and a few unpleasant things during their career. An-24 DDR-SBH ended its days in Vietnam, like most An-24s of Interflug. The two Tu-134s ended their days in Russia, flying for UTair and later the Gromov Flight Institute and the Tupolev Construction Bureau (DDR-SDH) and UTair and Tsentr-Yug, a small Russian carrier (DDR-SDI). Both have been permanently retired only quite recently.

After the fall of the Berlin Wall, and with nobody really knowing what was going to happen at least for a few weeks, TG-44 fell into a short period of Sleeping Beauty mode for a few months. Only in March 1990, flying resumed after a break of several months, as the GDR continued to exist for another half year, until October 3, 1990. The last (and only democratically-elected) prime minister of the GDR, Lothar de Maizière, was taken for a state visit to Washington onboard an Il-62 and on other state visits.

However, the end of the GDR, on October 3, 1990, also marked the end of this secretive squadron. When both Germanys became one, the assets of the GDR air force (including its aircraft and helicopters) were merged with the FRG's Luftwaffe. TG-44 and its Marxwalde base soon became part of Air Transport Squadron 65 (LTG 65), a unit of the air force overseeing all former GDR military aircraft and helicopters and their integration into an All-German Air Force.

Some of the VIP aircraft were transferred into the new squadron and operated in neutralized Interflug colours with the insignia of the German Air Force, such as the three Il-62s (DDR-SEN became 11+21, DDR-SEP 11+22 and DDR-SEV 11+20). They were mostly assigned to shuttle flights between the West German capital Bonn and Berlin, carrying members of government, state institutions and civil servants between two two cities (some 'normal' people were lucky enough to get a seat) and on select special missions.

But after the end of the GDR, its former government fleet were not put on high-level government flights any more, nor West Germany's four ageing Boeing 707-307C head of state transports. All were quickly replaced by the three former Interflug A310s.

TG44's three Il-62s were retired from use with the Luftwaffe in 1993. After their retirement, all three were temporarily stored at Manching Airport in southern Germany before being sold to newly-independent Uzbekistan's airline, and later passed on to Egyptian airline Alim Air, although only one seems to have entered service with the carrier as SU-ZDA, which ended its days at Cairo Airport. The other two Il-62s remained in Uzbekistan and are no longer flying. The two Il-62s previously operated by TG-44 were passed on to Interflug in 1984 (DDR-SEL) and 1987 (DDR-SEK), where they flew commercially, and even got the all-German "D-" registrations after the reunification (DDR-SEK became D-AOAE, DDR-SEL D-AOAF). Both were later sold to Aeroflot as CCCP-86562 and CCCP-86564. CCCP-86564 was involved in a ground collision with an Asiana Airlines Boeing 747 at Anchorage Airport in 1998 and later scrapped there.

The last three (of 26) Tu-134s made it into the Luftwaffe: 11+10 (ex DDR-SDR), 11+11 (previously DDR-SDS), and 11+12 (ex DDR-SDU). The two Tu-154s (maybe the best looking aircraft ever wearing the Interflug colours) became 11+01 and 11+02.

In 1993, LTG 65, the final incarnation of the TG-44, was officially liquidated and the squadron's history, one that its members and the GDR took great pride in, came to its end. Some of the pilots of TG-44 continued flying their aircraft when they were passed on to the Luftwaffe (quite a few had reservations about flying for what was their arch-enemy just a few months before). Others found jobs with commercial airlines and many chose entirely different careers. The airfield of Marxwalde is today known by its old name Neuhardenberg and is a sleepy general aviation airfield with some training aircraft based locally and hundreds of solar panels posted along both sides of its runway.

Interflug's crews: a privileged bunch?

Becoming a pilot or a flight attendant has been a dream for young people all over the world for as long as people have been flying. Living in a country like the GDR, where leaving the country and travelling was a privilege for very few, starting a career with Interflug was more than a dream, be it as a pilot or flight attendant. The attraction to see more of the world than most was immense, and to be accepted as a pilot or flight attendant was a jackpot win in life.

During the 1960s and 1970s, Interflug's network grew constantly and soon included destinations around Europe and, with the introduction of the Il-18 or later the Il-62, even further afield, in Africa, Asia and the Americas. All that average GDR citizens usually got to see of the world were socialist countries and even there were restrictions. Money was another matter – many simply could not afford to travel outside the country's borders or at all, regardless of political hurdles.

So Interflug became a symbol for wanderlust and the longing to see far away countries. A job as a pilot or stewardess at Interflug meant joining the most elitarian and privileged circles of East German society. The envy of friends and family was certain.

But even during times when pilots and flight attendants were in high demand, getting a foot in the door was never easy and applicants were turned upside down before being accepted, much more thoroughly than on airlines in other countries, because candidates did not only have to be physically and psychologically fit, they also had to be politically reliable and loyal citizens, ideally members of the party (essential for captains). Those who wanted to travel far away from the GDR had to be demonstrably patriotic and stand firmly on socialist ground with both feet.

Interflug crews were not only supposed to represent the GDR abroad with dignity, the government also wanted to make sure that they came back home from their flights. The government (and also the leadership of Interflug) had no illusions: visits to foreign (read: Western) countries had a very high level of attraction and the risk was that crew members would simply stay there, and seek asylum instead of returning to the GDR. Applicants knew what expectations were and prepared for their interviews carefully where questions could not only include topics like their motivation to become a pilot or flight attendant, but also details like what GDR leader Erich Honecker had said in a speech during his most recent state visit.

Apart from the actual job interview, candidates were up for a thorough background check. Relatives in West Germany, doubts about their political views, or even the slightest notion that a candidate could harbour a desire to defect from the GDR would result in the termination of their recruitment process. The government was quite aware of the frustration with travel restrictions among the general population and so, when allowing the privileged few to go abroad, the state needed to be extra careful. Anybody leaving the country and not returning was humiliating. The more reasons a person had not to permanently leave the GDR, the higher his or her chances to get accepted for a job interview.

The ideal profile: a party member, married, several children, no relatives in the West (and that was on top of the actual requirements for the job). Whatever kept the desire small to leave the country, for example a family, increased your chances to be accepted for the job.

The number of applicants was extremely high. The formal requirements for flight attendants (the vast majority female, until the end of the airline) included a high school degree, fluent mastering of at least two foreign languages (English-Russian or English-French) and a previous professional training were all essential. The training for the actual flight attendant job was extremely comprehensive and lasted around six months.

That you got accepted for the job as a pilot or flight attendant didn't mean that the entire world was waiting with open arms now. While anybody flying for Interflug had to be more than a loyal citizen, there was another division for crews. And this particular wall, an extension of the one encircling West Berlin, ran between ports designated either SW or NSW. Want to practice your German a bit? SW was the abbreviation for Sozialistischer Wirtschaftsraum, i.e. Socialist Economic Area.

NSW simply put a Nicht or Not in front of SW: Non-Socialist Economic Area. A small word, but a huge difference for Interflug's crew rosters. The (assumed) risk of somebody wanting to exchange their life in the GDR for one in Bulgaria, Hungary or the Soviet Union and

A pilot at work in an Ilyushin Il-18
Previous image: Why can she fly to Amsterdam and we can't?
Interflug Abteilung Werbung

permanently stay there was next to non-existent. Any GDR citizen could travel to those countries freely anyway, and thus all crew members were allowed to fly to these countries from day one.

But the temptation to work for the airline, of course, lay not in seeing Moscow or Sofia. In Europe, destinations like Helsinki, Amsterdam, Milan, Stockholm or Brussels would have seemed very tempting, not necessarily to stay there, but to get out and see the world beyond the Wall. Crews operating these flights were hand-picked and their number was to be kept as small as possible, to keep the risk of somebody defecting as low and controllable as possible. The occasional charter flights for sports teams and orchestras, and the torrent of flights to bring visitors from West German cities into the GDR for the annual Leipzig Trade Fair were on an even higher risk level. Some even had a layover in West Germany, so only the most inner cadres of loyal crews were allowed to fly them.

Before anyone was allowed to fly to NSW destinations, they had to prove themselves on SW routes, a process that could go on for many years, or if signs of sufficient political reliability were not demonstrated, forever. After joining Interflug, one was from that moment standing in line to get cleared to fly to the non-socialist ports.

And the organisation giving the green light, above anyone within Interflug, was ultimately the Ministry for State Security, known by its German initials as the Stasi. Extensive background checks took place, neighbours were interviewed, crew members had to fill in questionnaires listing their places of residence and contacts to relatives, including any beyond the national borders. Relatives in West Germany lowered chances of getting cleared significantly. One had to dissociate oneself from them and report any contact attempt from their side to the authorities.

And even if you did all that, the criteria according to how the selection was made often remained dubious and

Meanwhile, on the other side of the Il-18's cockpit door, cabin crew take care of the passengers
Interflug Abteilung Werbung

The Schönefeld tarmac doubles as a catwalk for Interflug's fashionable cabin crew
Interflug Abteilung Werbung
Previous page:
A captain briefs his first officer in the terminal at the beginning of another trip
Horst Sturm via Bundesarchiv

opaque. Sometimes, people were cleared to fly to non-socialist countries after a few years' time, sometimes never. No reason was given for either. And once you were cleared, that didn't mean that you didn't have to be careful. Small things could cost you your clearance (or even your job). One complete no-go was making contact with other crews or locals in non-socialist countries. More than a 'Good day' to a Lufthansa crew showing up at the hotel reception somewhere could get you in big trouble. The rules were hard and even the slightest change of your personal situation (a divorce or fresh romance) could result in a phone call: sorry, only socialist countries for you.

And hardly anyone in GDR society had more exposure to the temptations of the capitalist world, which led to a certain level of distrust between crew members. After all, in order to get reported to the supervisors, you need somebody to report you. It could be assumed that there were Stasi agents in every crew (and among passengers, too). So while one could usually guess, this was a big game of hide and seek.

After the reunification of the two Germanys, the Stasi files were opened to the public. One of the most disillusioning moments in the lives of many GDR citizens was the day they were able to see their Stasi file for the first time. More than often, the most trusted person in one's life was revealed as a Stasi member, or what was known as IM - Inoffizieller Mitarbeiter or unofficial collaborators who delivered private information to the authorities. Estimates are that there were around 189,000 of the latter towards the end of the GDR, all of them good friends, neighbours, colleagues, husbands or wives to somebody – or trusted fellow crew members.

For many crew, the temptation to leave the country was probably lower than the government feared. They were able to see the world (or at least more of it than 99% of the population of the GDR), enjoy their stroll through Milan or Paris, bring some perfume, a magazine or cigarettes back home and, knowing how privileged they were to be given this chance, were fine with it. After all, a home with your family, friends and social network is worth a lot, even though you know that not everything's perfect.

An interesting detail, which was practiced the same way at other airlines from Eastern Europe: before every flight from home base, all crew members had to see a doctor on the crewbase, who would typically ask you if you slept enough the night before, felt generally fit, and checked vital functions such as your blood pressure. This was also the time that the responsible flight attendant collected medical equipment for the flight, as it was not permanently loaded onboard aircraft.

As for rostering, small teams often flew together over and over again and became friends, sometimes more. One thing (of so many) that was not allowed officially, was romance between crew members. But of course it happened. Known romantic relations between colleagues could result in being banned from flying to the non-socialist world. The planning department tried to plan married couples on different flights where possible, at least on NSW trips, to minimize the risk of an escape attempt.

Things were not as glamourous and kitschy as displayed in the DEFA/Deutscher Fernsehfunk TV series Treffpunkt Flughafen (Meeting Point Airport) TV series, about a fictitious Interflug Il-62 crew, but probably quite comparable to the everyday life of an average airline crew today. In their day-to-day work, the knowledge that somebody within the crew was probably working for Stasi was put aside to achieve or maintain a positive atmosphere between colleagues.

The same was true for plainclothes security guards (Flugsicherheitsbegleiter) who were known to accompany almost all Interflug flights, even those to countries like Czechoslovakia or Poland, after a number of security incidents, most notably the hijacking of a LOT Tu-

Interflug Abteilung Werbung

134 en route from Gdansk, which, during final approach to land at Schönefeld, was commandeered by a GDR citizen and forced to instead polevault across the Berlin Wall and land at West Berlin's Tempelhof airport only one or two minutes flying time away. Concerns of copycat episodes also led to the cockpit door being closed for most visitors in an era where a visit to the flight deck during flight, both for grown ups and children, was perfectly normal on airlines elsewhere.

After the end of Interflug, some technical crew such as navigators and flight engineers were no longer needed in the modern cockpits of Western-built aircraft, and ended their career when Interflug ceased flying. The pilots and flight attendants continued flying for post-unification airlines like Condor, Lufthansa, LTU and Air Berlin. Others ended up further afield, such as in the Persian Gulf as the likes of Emirates, Etihad and Qatar Airways gathered momentum. Some continued flying for the German Air Force, which took over Interflug's three A310s and operates one of them to this day. Somewhere out there in the sky, Interflug's legacy flies on.

IF
Crew episodes

Marianne Jacobs-Dahlmann was one of the first flight attendants to fly for Deutsche Lufthansa, later Interflug, in the late 1950s. Having been trained as a forwarding agent, she joined the air cargo department of Deutsche Lufthansa at Schönefeld Airport. When flying operations started, ten girls from ground staff switched to domestic flying for an interim period of intially a few weeks.

She stayed on the job, joined and completed the second flight attendant training course and qualified to become a flight attendant on domestic and international routes. Even though it is very likely that a political background check was done for all applicants, it was done discretely. She was airborne on the Ilyushin Il-14 just a few weeks later. With 28 passenger seats (later increased to 32), only one flight attendant was rostered. The Il-18, the second type that Marianne flew, was crewed with three flight attendants, albeit all with the same rank – no one was designated as a superior, a purser. This took some adjustment – sometimes there were too many opinions, and working in a team of cabin crew was a new experience for flight attendants who had previously worked alone, running their own show and making their own decisions.

Today, more than half a century later, she recalls in particular the very busy domestic trips, often stretching over the entire country. Even though the GDR was small, six or even eight sectors made for very long days. Itineraries like Berlin-Leipzig-Berlin-Barth-Leipzig-Barth-Berlin-Leipzig-Berlin were absolutely common (Barth is a small town close to the Baltic Sea).

Sometimes, depending on the season, crews also overnighted in other cities in the GDR. Marianne enjoyed working on her own in the cabin. Even though service was more extravagant, she would say that, especially on domestic days, things were not really that different from today's work of a flight attendant.

Did politics play a role in her everyday life? Not a lot. While Marianne is certain that there were obstacles during the selection process, they were invisible. The same applied to being cleared to fly to capitalist countries. Some crews were allowed to fly to destinations outside the Warsaw Pact countries and some weren't, and the differentiating factor was obviously a question of trust by the authorities. But nobody knew what the requirements were or where the obstacles lay. And yes, she is certain that members of the Stasi were often among her passengers, but yet once more, it is a human quality to normalise or ignore doubts. At the end of the day, one can only look into somebody else's face and hope that he or she is a trustworthy person. Even though there was the occasional doubt about colleagues' background, she recalls her flights and the atmosphere onboard as amicable and trusting.

Not only the criteria for flying outside the socialist realm was opaque, but also the length of the process; some crew members were cleared almost immediately, and for others it took years to get a green light. And for some, it just never happened. Something that was accepted and not really questioned.

One of her favourite flights was from Berlin to Moscow. The Il-14 did not have the legs to fly Berlin-Moscow non-stop, so a stop in Vilnius was required. As the galley of the Il-14 was quite minimalistic, cold meals were supplied on even the shortest sectors but no hot meals were offered, even though they were expected by airline passengers of the era. The solution was that all passengers

Marianne during service on the Il-18
Previous page: Cabin service in the early days was very "manual", as there were no trolleys
Katja Rehfeld via Bundesarchiv

and the crew had their meal in the airport restaurant in Vilnius while their aircraft was being refuelled and replenished for the onward leg to Moscow (or back to Berlin). This lunch stop was always enjoyable, and responsibility for organising it including ordering food fell the flight attendant.

One cold winter day, Christmas just two days away, Marianne was assigned for a flight to Moscow, flight number DH600/601, Moscow via Vilnius, with takeoff from Schönefeld scheduled for 0600. She packed some winter boots into her ready-to-go suitcase and went off to catch the train from her home to Schöneweide S-Bahn station. From there, the so-called 'Pilot Bus' (also used by cabin crew) shuttled to the crew base at nearby Schönefeld.

It was still dark when passengers boarded the Il-14. The weather was crispy and cold but the forecast for the entire route to Moscow looked fine. Only five of the 28 seats remained empty (Marianne recalls that low passenger loads were rare). The pilots joked that they should not fly the Il-14 at maximum speed (only around 320 km/h anyway) as Marianne's mother was known around the airline to be terribly worried about her daughter and her wellbeing.

While the flight was yet to begin, Marianne's thoughts were already in Moscow, where the four crew members (three cockpit, one cabin) stayed in the airport hotel close to Vnukovo airport. It was a ritual to throw a dice to determine which of the four would travel into the city centre to buy Georgian tea, which came in beautiful coloured boxes, for the entire crew. When flying to the Soviet Union, crewmembers received an allowance in roubles. As the money could not be taken out of the country anyway, why not spend it and buy tea for everyone? Other than that, Moscow shopping was popular for books and vinyl records, and for similar reasons, Budapest was a hotspot for perfumes and lipsticks.

On trips to countries where the allowance was paid in hard, convertible currency, crews brought their own meals from home in order to save every penny of their allowance and bring it back home, as Western money was almost impossible to get in the GDR.

Were the crews privileged? "Of course!" says Marianne Jacobs-Dahlmann. "We had access to so many things that 'normal' people in the GDR could never get. And the privilege to travel abroad. Sofia or Budapest were better than nothing after all!"

After the usual break in the airport restaurant in Vilnius, the flight continued on to Moscow uneventfully. After landing at Vnukovo, Marianne shook every passenger's hand in farewell and the crew proceeded to the airport hotel for their rest. While December 23 is the peak of the pre-Christmas craziness in most European countries, it is a perfectly normal day in Russia, where big party is New Year, which is celebrated on January 6.

The next morning, temperatures were even lower in Moscow than in Berlin, at minus 16 degrees. The crew was eager to fly home, as Christmas Eve with their families was waiting. The Il-14 was parked next to several Aeroflot aircraft, plus CSA, SAS, and LOT. The passenger load was similar to the outbound flight, 23 to Vilnius and 17 on to Berlin. Marianne went to the airport terminal to order the meals. As she returned, the rest of the crew had put on sour faces. The aircraft's own little container of de-icing fluid had been emptied by someone overnight and, in addition, the hydraulic system seemed to be leaking. Berlin suddenly seemed light years away.

The flight was cancelled, passengers rebooked on other airlines, and the captain went to the control tower to get in touch with crew control and inform everybody's families that they wouldn't be home for Christmas. The crew returned disappointed to the airport hotel, and agreed on a little vodka reception in the hotel in the evening.

During layovers, Marianne remembers, crews often met for meals or drinks, but they were required to do so in uniform, a company rule at the time. That day, she prepared a little Christmas buffet for the crew with whatever catering she had been able to bring from the plane. She even 'stole' a little Christmas tree from the garden of the hotel without being noticed. Whatever she couldn't get (for example, a bottle of vodka), was organized by the 'floor lady' of the hotel, in return for a nice bottle of shampoo to be delivered during her next Moscow layover. And as it turned out, and in no small way because of Marianne's efforts, it was a very nice Christmas Eve. And one of several examples Marianne recalls of an almost family-like crew life in the early days of Lufthansa and Interflug.

While the GDR would have liked to have a 'Deutsche Lufthansa' as its flag carrier, the legal dispute over the name and brand rights with its West German counterpart were eventually lost. In order to be prepared for a (somewhat anticipated) defeat, the GDR founded Interflug, initially as a charter subsidiary. For some time, the two companies operated next to each other, some flights operated by Interflug, some by Lufthansa. There were even aircraft painted in the blue and white colours of Deutsche Lufthansa but sporting Interflug titles for some time. For the crews (who flew for both), this meant always checking their work roster carefully, as they all owned two sets of uniforms, one in a lighter tone of blue (Deutsche Lufthansa) and a darker one for Interflug.

Marianne Jacobs-Dahlmann's career with Interflug ended quite abruptly, when in 1961, before the Berlin Wall was built, she left the GDR for Karlsruhe in West Germany together with her then-fiancé.

Hannelore Mildes was another former Interflug / Deutsche Lufthansa flight attendant of the early days and I was lucky enough to speak to her about her career with the airline. Unfortunately, at 87 years old, Hannelore passed away in May 2022. She was among the first flight attendants ever flying for what was still Deutsche Lufthansa. Hannelore spent part of her childhood in Georgia and after finishing school, she studied foreign languages at the Karl Marx University in Leipzig, perhaps the most prestigious linguistic institute in the GDR. With a future posting (there was not always a free choice) at the GDR's embassy in Moscow looming, something she was absolutely not looking forward to, one day an interesting visit occurred at the university. A couple of recruiters from Deutsche Lufthansa visited the university to recruit cabin attendants from the ranks of the female students. Languages (most notably English and Russian) were a prerequisite for candidates, and as the airline was not yet in the air, there was no stream of applicants yet.

Potential recruits understood little of this new job opportunity and thus, representatives of the airline went about to look for suitable candidates. Hannelore was a bit shy and maybe didn't raise her arm high enough; the first batch of six flight attendants did not include her. But when the recruiters returned to the university, Hannelore's desire to avoid the Moscow posting drove her to sign up. Fortunately, recruiting new flight attendants for the nascent airline was a higher priority for the government than staffing their embassies, and she joined the second batch intake of six.

What did the training look like in these early days? "Well," she says, "There was pretty much none." Deutsche Lufthansa was only just getting started, with hardly any administration, let alone a training centre. The provisional headquarters and facilities were in Diepensee, a small town south of Schönefeld airport. As the first Il-14s were yet to arrive, there was no aircraft to even train future cabin attendants on.

Service training was mostly done at upscale restaurants in Berlin, where the new flight attendants learned proper service and hospitality (although the service provided in a good restaurant had very little to do with the inflight service on a rugged Il-14 on a bumpy and short flight from Berlin to Prague). Medical training was given to the new flight attendants at Berlin's famous Charité hospital where, as Hannelore recalls, they even assisted with several births (well, with dolls, not with real women). A lot of theoretical training including meteorology followed, and the total course took about half a year.

In the early days of the operation, with few flights, new cabin crew were put to work in ground-based roles, in customer service or answering phone calls at the information desk. During the first months of Deutsche Lufthansa, cockpit crews were all Russians, so on an Il-14, there were four Russian guys in the cockpit and one German girl working in the cabin.

Looking back, Hannelore and many of her colleagues remember the first weeks and months of flying, when things were fairly improvised, as the best days of her flying career. Being a flight attendant myself, I can concur that unusual situations, where hardly anything goes according to the book and you have to improvise, are the most challenging the moment they happen but also the most rewarding when looking back. When they were first put into service with Deutsche

Lufthansa, the Il-14s only had 18 seats, quite a luxurious configuration! The entire crew usually met 90 minutes before flight departure, went to the air traffic control and weather service together (weather conditions played a much greater role on the low-flying Il-14 than on later types like the Il-18 and Il-62). All crew members had to undergo a brief medical check-up, with their temperature and blood pressure checked, and the cabin attendant was given their personal medical kit for first aid on board.

Once onboard the aircraft, the flight attendant had to replace seat covers for all the seats, stock seat pockets with sickness bags, and replenish bathroom supplies. Back in those days, passengers were generously fed on flights, so catering service was loaded, consisting of the so-called 'onboard buffet' plus ten thermos bottles filled with hot coffee and tea. There were no standardised trolleys or boxes, so again, everything was quite improvised. When the flight got bumpy (which was often), there was quite a mess.

The airsick bags were also put to good use; Hannelore Mildes recalls that on the Il-14 in particular and its low cruising altitude, there was a lot of throwing up by passengers. During a time of delivery shortages for the laminated paper sickbags, transparent plastic bags had to be used for a while, which had a bit of an 'encouraging' effect on seat mates. Ah, the glamour of flying!

A typical flight on the Il-14 in the early days was Berlin-Prague-Budapest-Sofia followed by an overnight stay in Sofia. When the flight was full, the flight attendant was more than busy. On the first leg to Prague, service included delicious waffles, a choice of drinks, cigarettes (yes!) and pralinés. On the second leg from Prague to Budapest, everybody was given a cold meal tray, a choice of drinks, a praliné box, more cigarettes, and Deutsche Lufthansa-branded matches and cognac. Among passengers, in its early days Deutsche Lufthansa was sometimes called 'Cognacdampfer', the Cognac Steamer, and apparently when given a choice, some chose Deutsche Lufthansa over other carriers because of its very good service or the desirability of these gifts. On the third leg to Sofia, the opulent service of the second leg was repeated once more. Passengers were indeed very well fed and watered. (The Il-14 was later upgraded to a more efficient 26 seats, which meant even more work for the flight attendant and less of that first class experience for passengers.)

Hannelore remembers vividly that the Il-14 did not have a microphone or

Service during the early days was more personal than today. This is Hannelore Mildes serving a fresh cup of tea.

public address system, so she virtually had to shout her announcements at passengers once the noisy engines were running. This was an important role as passengers back in those days were a lot more interested in the routing of the flight and what could be seen along the way, often including a bit about the history of a particular region or city that was being overflown. After a while in the job, she knew exactly where in the cabin she had to position herself to make herself heard, but that meant doing the same announcements time and time again, as, more than a few metres away, people would simply not hear her.

With airsick passengers, shouted geography lessons, and the provision of a lavish service without trolleys, all performed at low and often bumpy altitudes, three flights could leave you quite exhausted. But apparently, there was still time for romance. Although this was frowned upon by the company (new employees, at least during the early days, actually signed agreements that they would not get involved with passengers or colleagues), but of course romance was in the air. These things just happen, just as they do today. Even when it did not lead to a relationship, there was the occasional overture from passengers. Two of the most remarkable gifts she received were a big Salami from a Hungarian guest and a cocker spaniel puppy.

Hannelore met her future husband on a flight, but in the early days of their romance, like others in a similar position, they had to be secretive about their relationship. Of course, colleagues would be speculating and gossiping, but everybody was pretty good at covering things up. And in true aircrew style, the wedding almost got cancelled, as she was stuck in Vilnius for five (!) quite chaotic days because of fog.

Once she and her husband wore their wedding rings and made the whole thing official (they were the first known Deutsche Lufthansa marrieds, at least among crews), company management was basically fine with it. But one limitation remained for the existence of Deutsche Lufthansa and later Interflug:

Interflug Abteilung Werbung

couples were never rostered on the same flights, in particular when these went to countries outside the Iron Curtain; the risk of couples defecting was perceived to be too high. By leaving their partner back in the GDR, possibly even with a family and a home, this seemed much less likely. But, at the end of the day, as Hannelore explains, this fear was largely unsubstantiated. "We all had our homes and families, and our lives as flight crew were very privileged compared to the average people who couldn't travel or have access to goods from overseas, so the temptation to actually leave all this behind for what would have been an uncertain future in a strange country was not very tempting for most."

After a maternity break of three years (her granddaughter is a flight attendant with the German Air Force today, so this really is an aviation family), Hannelore returned to her flying duties when the airline's transition from Deutsche Lufthansa to Interflug was in full swing and both brands were operating side by side. Like Marianne Jacobs-Dahlmann, she had to choose her uniform accordingly – light blue or dark blue. In 1969, she swapped her flying career for an office job, dealing with contracts, accounting and relations with other airlines.

She stayed with the airline right until the end, actually even beyond that. When the decision was made to liquidate Interflug, she was elected to help bring employees into new jobs, putting them into training schemes and generally be of assistance. Her employer in this final phase was the Treuhand Agency, the state branch dealing with the liquidation of so many companies of the GDR. Helping to liquidate your own company was not major fun, but Hannelore, one of the first to join, was also among the last to leave.

After portraying Hannelore Mildes and Marianne Jacobs-Dahlmann, the last cabin crew member we meet is quite a bit younger than the two ladies. André Skrabania, born in 1969, was in one of the last attendants to be trained for Interflug service, joining the airline in January 1990.

André wanted to be a flight attendant for as long as he can remember but his first attempt to join Interflug in the early 1980s wasn't successful. Not to be dissuaded, he decided to learn a trade first, studying mechanical engineering, then completed his military service and then ended up working in the state travel agency, the Haus des Reisens (House of Travel) in Berlin's Alexanderplatz. Most employees had specialised in one

André making a PA announcement on the Tu-134

country and for André it was Poland. As the Interflug main sales office was virtually next door in the same building, he befriended some of the staff working there, and got wind of the airline looking for flight attendants in the late 1980s. Time to give it another try!

Until the early 1980s, male flight attendants were quite a rarity at Interflug, although there were always a handful. On some of the earlier aircraft, cabin service was actually hard physical work. Cabin crew had to get service items from a storage area in the cabin, unload, re-stow. Trolleys and standardised boxes that speed up cabin service today were unheard of and thus, a strong man in the crew was always appreciated. Many of the early male flight attendants were actually recruited from Interflug's maintenance department and were former technicians.

André's second attempt to become a flight attendant was a success and training started in early 1990, the vacuum between the fall of the Berlin Wall and the reunification of both Germanys. For the GDR population and also for Interflug crews, these were optimistic times. Overnight, they could travel everywhere, buy everything and become part of the rest of the world, oblivious of Interflug's liquidation just a year in the future.

The optimism reached the upper echelons of Interflug management, who looked to new markets and new opportunities, hence the new cabin crew intake. Three flight attendant courses started at the same time, and their duration was reduced from almost six months to just two (typical for today). All the political and civic elements that had been a staple of the course were chopped, leaving just emergency, medical and service training in place.

André's first flight was on March 4, 1990, to Larnaca. The destination was quite sensational. Previously, Interflug's crews were divided into those who could only fly to socialist countries, and those privileged few who were deemed politically reliable enough to fly to the rest of the world. With the political changes that had just occured, these categories were a thing of the past.

Instead of the usual five flight attendants on the Il-62, André was onboard as an additional crew member (ACM), flight attendant number six. The Il-62 was one of only two aircraft types he was trained on, the other being the Tu-134. (The Il-18 and the Airbus A310 fleets were full crewed.) His first 'real' on-duty flight after all training was finished was on the friendship line to Moscow, on another Il-62.

The Il-62 remained his favourite aircraft to work on. It was spacious and had one decisive advantage over the short haul Tu-134: layovers. Within months of joining the airline, André flew with it to Singapore, Bangkok, Maputo and Havana. Layovers in sunny climes is one of the benefits of this job.

After German reunification, many contracts the GDR had with befriended socialist countries came to an end. Many of the GDR's companies were liquidated after reunification and workers employed from abroad were no longer needed. Foreign students and scientists were in a similar situation. Many were flown back to their home countries on repatriation flights (this article was written during the early weeks of the Covid-19 crisis and some parallels could be felt).

André remembers one particular trip when a crew was sent to Nairobi (deadheading on Lufthansa, how times had suddenly changed!). There, they were based for 14 days and took over

Il-62s arriving from Berlin and operated shuttle flights to Mozambique and back to Nairobi every two or three days, enjoying safaris and other African adventures in the meantime.

The euphoric mood of early 1990 changed rapidly when Interflug, like most other companies in the GDR, was put under the administration of the Treuhand. Within four years, Treuhand sold around 50,000 properties, almost 10,000 companies, and more than 25,000 small businesses, often at ridiculously low prices, or simply closed them. Initially, it seemed like a partnership with Lufthansa or British Airways could be created, but in the end, this did not happen.

Like many other Interflug employees, André learnt about the Treuhand's decision to liquidate the airline in February 1991 from the newspaper. The remaining weeks required very little flying for crew as the flight programme was drastically reduced: the Il-62 was almost completely taken out of service leaving the Tu-134 fleet, the A-310s, and the sole Dash-8. André's last on-duty flight was in late April 1991, a roundtrip to Milan on the Tu-134.

After the end of Interflug, employees were put in a transfer company, still receiving their salary for a few months, and offered several different training schemes that would make them fit to apply for other jobs. Flight attendants were given generic flight attendant training (provided by a Lufthansa subsidiary), and could apply for a job as cabin crew with Lufthansa, Lufthansa CityLine, or Condor.

For André, Lufthansa was the goal, for its scale of operation and route map. However, true to his career path thus far, a little detour was to be expected. His application was rejected, but he found a job with subsidiary Lufthansa CityLine and flew the Fokker 50, Canadair Regional Jets and Avroliners from iconic Tempelhof Airport. What a contrast to the mighty Il-62 and Tu-134 from Schönefeld! Later, Andre joined Condor based in Frankfurt and flew their fleet of Boeing 757s and 767s, and the DC-10.

Finally, in 2005, André became a flight attendant for Lufthansa. Today he is based in Munich and is trained on the whole Airbus fleet – A320, A330, A340, A350, A380. Although his time with Interflug was short, he has fond memories. Working for a major airline today, even after 15 years with the company it is possible to fly with a crew of total strangers, so he misses the days of Interflug, where basically everybody knew each other's name and felt like part of a big family.

Although Interflug is long gone, André is one of the most passionate preservers of the airline's legacy, publishing a calendar highlighting the airline's different aircraft types each year (please have a look at www.reprowings.com), and is one of the driving forces voluntarily running and maintaining Il-62 DDR-SEG in the village of Stölln.

The author (a flight attendant himself) is jealous: flight attendants working on a Tu-134 (André is the guy in the middle)

Solidarity flights and charter work

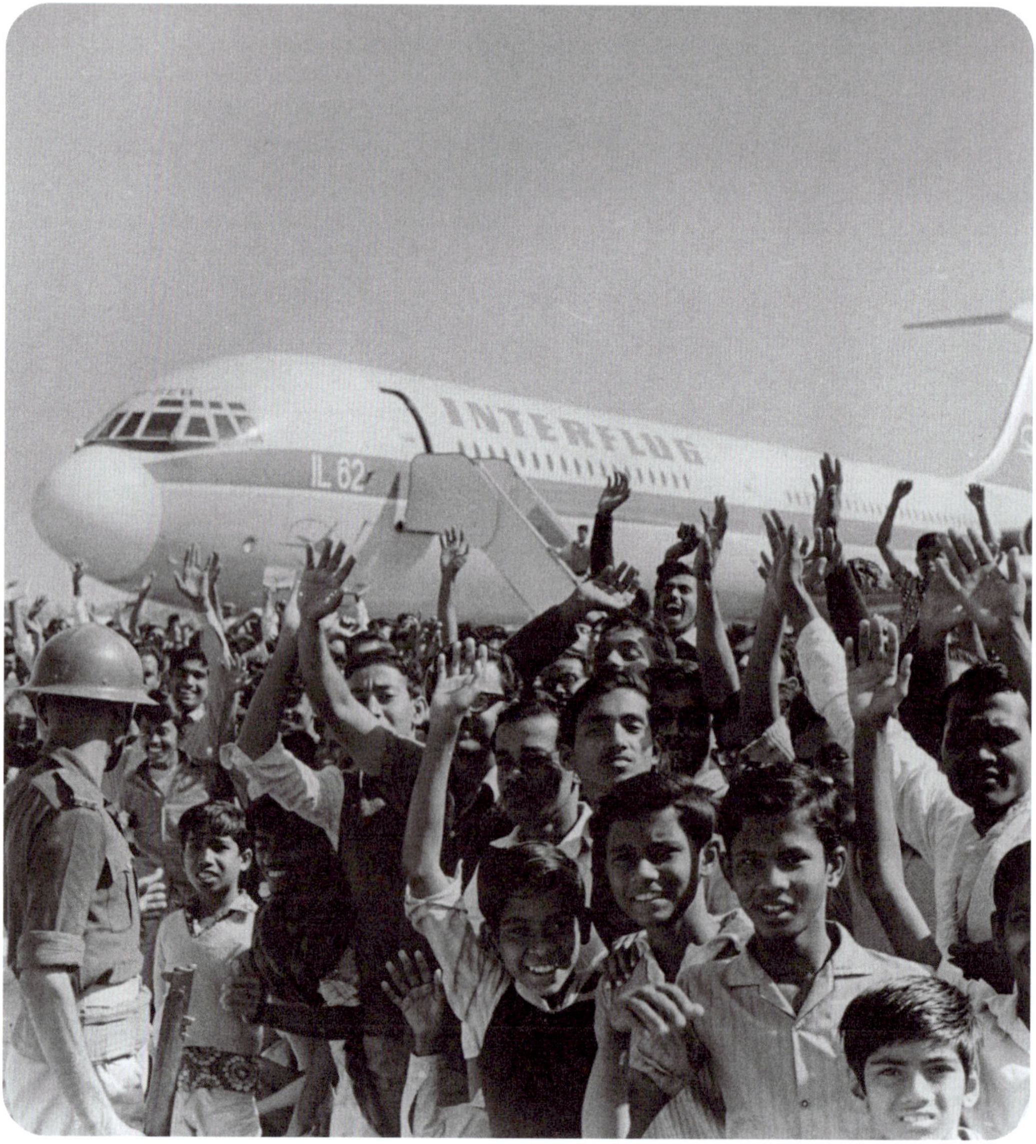

It is safe to say that the society of the GDR was more compassionate, where solidarity with others played a bigger role in every day life, than in other countries. That was true both on a personal level with your neighbours and on the highest government level with fellow socialist nations in need. Solidarity was an indispensable part in everyday life and on a personal level, people tried to help each other out where they could. And it is one aspect from the GDR that many former citizens miss today.

International solidarity with other (befriended) countries on government level also played a role, even though sometimes political influence, strategic interests of the nation may have been a more immediate motivation than the actual act of solidarity. Many countries newly independent of their old colonial masters; the GDR helped out, not only with political support but also by supplying goods such as school materials to food to more weapons and ammunition produced in the GDR. As soon as the GDR had its own aircraft fleet (and be that civilian aircraft operated by Deutsche Lufthansa and later Interflug, planes operated by the National People's Army, or the secretive Transportgeschwader 44 later on), these were used for what were universally known as solidarity flights.

For most of the GDR's existence, Interflug had the most capable aircraft fleet, hence, by government order, the airline and its aircraft were often assigned to very unusual and often dangerous missions in remote areas of the world. The Il-18 played a big role as it had long range, but with excellent short field performance and rough field capability. Translation: it could fly in and out of anywhere including war zones.

Interflug often ended up operating flights that should have been the natural preserve of the GDR military but for a long time, the air force did not have an aircraft type appropriate to the mission. Missions were often assigned at very short notice, and, whether a single flight or a long trip of several weeks abroad, the crew usually received very little information about the cargo, and whether the trip was operating for humanitarian reasons or out of commercial interests, and the sometimes explosive nature of their missions (quite literally). The more high-profile the mission, the more likely that a high-level government or party representative was onboard to accompany the flight and pose for pictures, as these flights made for excellent public relations all round.

There was a strong feeling of pride and achievement among those crews operating solidarity flights, so risks and delays were quite readily accepted. Participants were also often awarded with medals or other insignia of glory and gratefulness by the government or

An injured sandinist on his way from Nicaragua to Berlin for medical treatment
Dr. Heinz Frotscher via Bundesarchiv
Previous image: A solidarity flight is met by locals at Calcutta Airport in January 1972
Hubert Link via Bundesarchiv

party for their efforts. For the everyday operation of Interflug, these missions often meant major disruptions, as aircraft and crews would suddenly become unavailable for regular flying duties, sometimes for a lengthy period, and at very short notice.

The first solidarity flight took place almost as early as Interflug (or Deutsche Lufthansa at the time) was up and running as an airline. In January 1958, Ilyushin Il-14 DM-SAB, took off from Berlin Schönefeld, destination Hanoi – not exactly a short trip for an Il-14. The aircraft was loaded with school material, clothes and toys for the children of Vietnam, following a donation campaign in the GDR. After more than 33 hours flying time and numerous stops on the way, the crew was given an overwhelming reception at Hanoi Airport and even received by Ho Chi Minh personally.

Almost all corners of the world saw solidarity flights over the decades and the network flown by charter services by Interflug exceeded their route map of scheduled flights by far. Ever since they joined the fleet in 1960, Interflug's Il-18s were the aircraft type of choice for these unusual flights. They were the most flexible and versatile aircraft and could operate a scheduled Budapest service in the morning, fly baby chickens to Baghdad overnight and then go on a lengthy mission to a remote part of the world before carrying tourists to the Black Sea a few days later. No other aircraft in Interflug's fleet or the entire GDR's aircraft inventory could do what the Il-18 could. The Il-18's flexibility and consequent high regard by Interflug's team could be part of the reason that the fleet was the only part of the airline that survived the airline's demise, at least for a while, as Berline.

Destinations for solidarity flights included Mongolia, Angola, Nicaragua, Mozambique, Vietnam, Yemen, Bangladesh or Pakistan, and the character of the missions could not have been more diverse. Some examples: in July 1973, youth delegations from various African countries were flown to Tunis for a Panafrican Meeting. In the same month, food and relief supplies were on their way to Bamako (Mali), Addis Ababa (Ethiopia) and Ouagadougou (Burkina-Faso) courtesy of Interflug.

Two months later, relief supplies were carried to Lahore in Pakistan after severe floods there. In November 1973, practically a scheduled solidarity route to Vietnam was inaugurated (with the Vietnam war its decisive phase).

A bit later, in spring 1974, repatriation flights were operated from Bangladesh to Pakistan following the separation of the two countries, which had been East and West Pakistan, which had from 1953 until 1971 both been governed by Karachi (Islamabad from 1967). Dhaka would later be a scheduled stopover, as newly independent Bangladesh found friends and trading partners on both sides of the Iron Curtain, including the GDR.

Interflug aircraft were occasionally leased out to carry fraternal heads of state like Nicaragua's Daniel Ortega (who incidentally is back in the presidency today) and Palestinian leader Yassir Arafat.

Afghanistan became a regular destination for Interflug-operated aid flights in the 1980s in support of the Soviet Union's invasion, which lasted almost the entire decade and cost over one million lives, including 15,000 Soviet personnel. (Many believe the high cost in blood and treasure of the Soviet Union's Afghan adventure played a role in the collapse of the USSR in 1991.) Flights to Kabul, usually operated by Il-18 with an en-route stop in Tashkent, became a

Arrival of a solidarity flight in Beirut in 1976   via Bundesarchiv

The aircraft type most commonly used for solidarity flights and other special missions was the Il-18
Alan Bushell

regular occurence, carrying anything from clothes and medical supplies to printing presses (helping to print school books locally). These flights were particularly risky, as there was always the risk of being shot at during the challenging approach into Kabul Airport.

This was not Interflug's first encounter with Afghanistan. Quite remarkably, in 1976, an Interflug Tu-134 was chartered by West Germany's air rescue service to repatriate a group of West German tourists that had been injured in a bus accident, from Kabul to Berlin by Tu-134.

Even though theses special missions came with a lot of risk, very little ever happened. The saddest exception is the crash of Il-18 DM-STL during a take-off accident at the Angolan capital of Luanda on March 26, 1979, the only loss of an Il-18 for Interflug during flight (sister ship DM-STF was destroyed during a fire in a maintenance hangar in Moscow in 1967). The aircraft had been temporarily based in Luanda carrying supplies and weapons to Lusaka in support of the Zambian independence movement. The Il-18's good safety record with Interflug shows not only the robustness of this aircraft but also the high level of professionalism of Interflug's crews.

Interflug's cockpit crews got used to flying to very unusual parts of the world and the cabin crews to serving regular passengers one day and holding the little hands of traumatized children (or grown-up refugees) that were flown to the GDR for medical treatment or recovery or repatriated to other countries as an act of international solidarity.

The most time-consuming mission in the service of humanity for Interflug's crews (and probably the most memorable and physically as well as psychologically demanding one) was in the Horn of Africa in the 1980s. Following years of drought and mismanagement, Ethiopia was suffering from a major famine. Eventually, the Ethiopian government called upon other countries for help. Up to four GDR aircraft at a time (two National People's Army Antonov An-26 and two Interflug Il-18) were based at the airports of Assab (now in Eritrea) on the Red Sea, and landlocked Dire Dawa, beginning in November 1984 and lasting for almost a whole year.

Most humanitarian goods arrived in the port of Assab by ship and needed to be re-distributed. With little to no ground infrastructure, getting the precious cargo to other places where it was needed was perhaps the most challenging task in the face of the disaster that had befallen the country, and something that Ethiopia itself was not able to even remotely achieve at the time.

Here, two commercial airlines (one of them Interflug, the other, US charter outfit Transamerica, operating a fleet of Hercules) and numerous air forces from countries like the USSR, Sweden, the UK, Poland, Bulgaria, the United States teamed up in a major international effort to stop the hunger. Transalls operated by the West German Luftwaffe also took part and it was here in Ethiopia that the crews of Interflug, the GDR's National People's Army, and the West German Air Force got closer than they had anywhere else before. Contact between the crews, however, stayed very limited (mostly because the GDR government, fed

Erich Honecker arriving in Cuba for a state visit in 1974   Joachim Spremberg via Bundesarchiv

intelligence by members of the travelling party, would not have been very happy) but those who took part in it remember it as a very professional and almost friendly co-operation.

Assab Airport, the main hub of the emergency operation, was a tiny airfield. At the time, it received one scheduled flight per week and was absolutely not up to the mission of suddenly handling dozens of aircraft carrying several hundred tons of cargo every day. Its runway was too short, the apron not strong enough to carry the weight of some of the aircraft and there was only a single fuel truck that was sometimes broken. In pictures from the time, you can see an Interflug Il-18 with the landing gear partly sunk into the desert sand. Conditions got worse at even smaller airfields around Ethiopia, some just football pitches, with very basic infrastructure and no navigational aids.

Even the most experienced fliers sometimes reached their limits. During their time in Ethiopia, Interflug's crews recorded more landings and take-offs in one month than they would usually accumulate in half a year flying the line back home.

And even though it was a civilian airline, Interflug's crews were under military (GDR) command in Africa. Before landing at a new airport (during the entire mission, Interflug and the National People's Army landed at more than 15 different airfields around the country), the pilots routinely did a few test approaches and low passes to investigate the conditions close-up, checking runway length and condition, and for any possible obstacles (sometimes camels). Information about the provisionary airfields was often unreliable and which is why cockpit crews went to look for themselves before actually touching down there.

On a first flight, to play it safe, the only aircraft carried a fraction of the maximum load of the aircraft. When landing anywhere, the aircraft were usually greeted by hundreds or thousands of locals waiting for much-needed supplies.

The mission in Ethiopia put an enormous strain on aircraft, flight crews and perhaps most of all on the people working on the ground, such as the accompanying technicians. The pilots could at least get away from the searing heat – up to 50 degrees in the Red Sea town of Assab – once airborne, but ground crews had to live with it. Every four to six weeks, crews flew back home for a month, only to come back to Ethiopia again a bit later.

While most of the flights carried grain or other food supplies, some of them flew passengers, too. There were many repatriation flights, bringing Ethiopians from parts of the country most severely affected by the drought, to more fertile areas. The passengers were, of course, all first-time fliers, most of them mothers and their little kids. Interflug's Il-18s were usually only used as freighters in Ethiopia, so they did not have passenger seats. Safety nets were stretched across the cabin when passengers were flown. It is very unlikely that any of them ever forgot the first flight of their lives.

Almost needless to say: all aircraft involved in the operation in Ethiopia got back home safely and without any serious incidents. The successful operation of even the most tricky aid missions gained Interflug a very good reputation in the troublespots of the world as a reliable and safe operator.

And compared to Western airlines, they were usually a lot cheaper, too. This paid off commercially for the carrier and resulted in some lucrative

Because of its range, the Il-62 was often used for government missions and special flights on other continents.
Jacques Guillem

charter contracts, for example on behalf of a chicken farm from Austria, carrying hundreds of thousands of baby chickens to Iran and Iraq. Chicken flights, often carrying more than 100,000 little baby chicks, became a good revenue source for the airline for a while.

For decades, Interflug also operated regular charter flights on behalf of the country's fishing fleets, to Iceland, Canada, Scotland, Uruguay and Argentina and Angola, swapping trawler crews every 90 days and thus securing the GDR's fish supplies.

Or on behalf of the oil industry; between 1975 and 1978, Interflug (and the National People's Army) flew thousands of workers between the GDR and the Ukraine, who were together building the so-called Druzhba oil pipeline, crucial for the country's supplies of oil from the Soviet Union.

The term 'solidarity flight' was pretty elastic and could also mean supporting the commercial airlines of fellow socialist countries when they asked for help: between November 1976 and April 1977, Interflug operated all domestic flights on behalf of CSA Czechoslovak Airlines with an Il-18 as the airline had a temporary aircraft shortage. Socialist solidarity!

The solidarity flights to all corners might have been a logistics headache for Interflug operationally, but for the GDR, they were an important tool to not only support countries in need but also help to achieve political and commercial goals. The regular use of Interflug for missions that would have been more suitable for an air force also show how the airline, a civilian carrier on paper, was instrumental as a political tool by the government, often for very good causes but not universally so. And while the commercial aspect of flying became more and more important towards the end of the airline, true solidarity missions continued to some degree right up until the end of the airline.

The first German low-cost airline

Throughout Interflug's existence, charter flights played an important role for the airline (most notably for the balance sheet). Some had a political origin (acts of solidarity with fellow communist countries) but most had really only one intention: generate much-needed Western currency for the GDR. Interflug tried to secure whatever charter deal paid in hard currency they could get, and that sometimes took operations to the limit.

Another target to generate additional revenue (and hard currency) were, although this may seem a bit opportunistic, passengers from West Berlin (and other parts of West Germany). In the 1960s, 1970s and 1980s, the world of commercial aviation was highly regulated. Fares were often astronomically high compared to today, determined by IATA for all their members. One of the few airlines that was not a member was Interflug (the airline only joined the club in July 1990, months before ceasing operations). Being able to offer more flexible and cheaper fares than IATA members opened quite a few business opportunities for Interflug. During the division of Germany, only British, French and American airlines were allowed to serve West Berlin's Tempelhof, and later Tegel airports, and the pilots of the craft had to be citizens of those countries. British Airways, Air France, Pan Am and one or two niche players (Air-Berlin USA, Dan-Air London) had made themselves very comfortable in their cozy monopoly situation, usually charging passengers the full IATA fares with very few special offers ever available.

Not being an IATA member, Interflug was not bound by the cartel's fares and able to offer cheaper prices. And when hard currency was to be made, why not make it with travel-hungry West Berliners, just down the street from Schönefeld Airport? For most GDR citizens, travelling by plane remained a dream, as travel restrictions put most countries off-limits, and tickets were expensive. Their world remained very small, and that was one of the biggest frustrations for many. Even a ticket to nearby destinations like Prague or Budapest cost at least half a month's salary.

At the same time, Interflug served a number of destinations in the capitalist world and one of the airline's tasks was to generate hard currency. A way to do that, when domestic demand was not very high, was to fill flights with lucrative passengers from West Germany. And it was a win-win situation, because for them, the fares that Interflug offered were much lower than what they would usually pay for flights originating in West Berlin. When some Deutschmarks could be saved, people didn't mind travelling long distances and often went to great lengths to fly Interflug.

In order to make things as straightforward as possible as possible for passengers from West Berlin, in 1963 a special border checkpoint was installed close to Schönefeld Airport, at Waltersdorfer Chaussee, the most southeasterly point of West Berlin, in the locality of Rudow, just a few metres away from the airport terminal. Passengers flying from Schönefeld could board regular Ikarus shuttle busses from West Berlin's central bus terminal close to the Trade Fair at a cost of five D-Marks. After crossing at the border post nearby, it was a short drive to Schönefeld Airport, where they could check in for their flight just like everybody else (although at separate counters). By 1984, more than 300,000 travellers used the border crossing annually, most of them before or following a flight from Schönefeld. This number illustrates the volume of passengers that Interflug generated in West Berlin. At the time, the carrier carried shy of 1.5 million passengers a year. Passengers from West Berlin meant serious business! Other than for airline passengers going to Schönefeld Airport, this border checkpoint was not very well-known and saw very little use.

In 1985, procedures were simplified further. A whole terminal section (Terminal B) was opened for passengers travelling to and from West Berlin by bus. The area was sealed off from the other parts of the terminal building both inside the terminal as well as on the large forecourt outside and could only be reached by a checkpoint with a barrier. The feeder buses from West Berlin were then no longer checked at the nearby border crossing (Waltersdorfer Chaussee). Instead, a member of the passport control units of the GDR border troops boarded there and accompanied the short trip to Terminal B, making sure that no GDR citizen could board the bus during this part of the journey and thus enter the "West Area" of the airport unnoticed. Check-in, baggage claim as well as passport control of West Berlin passengers also took place separately. It was only in the main departure hall that they joined the "general" (East German) passengers. On arrival, the procedure was reversed: from 1985 onwards, passengers to West Berlin no longer had to enter the general arrivals area, were instead directed to a separate arrivals area in Terminal B, not without their passports being strictly checked first. There, they boarded the transit bus, once again accompanied by a member of the border patrol units. At the border post, the inspector left the bus and released the bus into West Berlin without further controls. This simplified procedure made using flights from Schönefeld, on Interflug or other carriers, an even more attractive option for travellers from the West.

While Interflug was the biggest airline in Schönefeld, other carriers serving the airport benefitted from passengers originating from the Western part of the city, too. Finnair, Turkish Airlines, Austrian, SAS and KLM (not to mention carriers from Eastern Bloc countries like Cubana, Malev, CSA of Czechoslovakia, or Aeroflot) all served the airport and while extreme bargains were mostly to be made on airlines of the Eastern Bloc, flights on other airlines at Schönefeld gave passengers more options when travelling from Berlin. In the end, each airline followed their own interests and airlines like Malev, Balkan or Aeroflot tried to compete with Interflug's fares where they could.

Interflug and Schönefeld Airport were very popular with the big Turkish diaspora living in West Berlin. When Interflug and Turkish Airlines (who also flew to Schönefeld) agreed that only the two of them were allowed to transport passengers between Turkey and Schönefeld, this produced outrage with Balkan, Czech Airlines or Malev, who also hoped to generate much-needed Western currency with these passengers. As a small retaliation, these carriers then ignored previously made pricing agreements with Interflug and undercut the airline on other routes. Airlines operating from Tegel Airport were not very happy about the cheap alternative nearby, and neither were West Berlin politicians who sensed treason and appealed to their upright fellow citizens to only use Tegel Airport for their travels. In the end however, there was not much they could do. Even PR campaigns supporting Tegel Airport largely went up in smoke and many passengers made their choice according to ticket price.

Sometimes more, sometimes less visible, both German governments lobbied hard to make life a bit more difficult for the respective other side. When American charter airlines like Modern Air offered charter flights to Bulgaria from Tegel Airport, the GDR intervened by (temporarily) revoking Bulgarian traffic rights at Schönefeld. The same happened when Interflug, maybe a bit prematurely, advertised a new route to Las Palmas in the Canary Islands in 1982, to be served by Ilyushin Il-62, totally focussed on passengers from West Berlin. Just a few days later, the West German government announced it had not granted Interflug landing or overflight rights for this service and intended to keep it that way. Nice little skirmishes along the way...

Apart from scheduled flights, where destinations and frequencies were increasingly selected according to demand from Western customers, Interflug also entered directly into agreements with tour operators from West Berlin like Unger Flugreisen or Berliner Flug-Ring for numerous charter flights, mostly to the usual sunshine destinations around the Mediterranean. Dozens of travel agencies in West Berlin (and also other German cities) specialised on bargain fares with Interflug or other Eastern European carriers from Schönefeld, so for more than two decades, Schönefeld became an Eldorado for those looking for cheap fares. Interflug's sales office at Friedrichstraße railway station in the city (an important transfer point between East and West Berlin) was accessible to travellers from West Berlin wishing to buy a ticket on the carrier, although on GDR territory.

Although the GDR government was not keen on its citizens mixing with Westerners at all, that was a situation that could not be avoided onboard a plane. And while Westerners stayed among themselves (except for the crew) on charter flights operated on behalf of West-German tour operators, passengers from East and West Germany mixed on scheduled Interflug flights, in the vast majority of cases meeting citizens of the 'other' Germany for the first time.

It is no exaggeration to say that Interflug was an early-day low-cost airline (at least for travellers from the West), enjoying strong political support from the government, maybe comparable to the legendary early Icelandair transatlantic flights from Luxemburg to Iceland and the United States.

Page 102: Happy passengers boarding a charter flight to Mallorca at Dresden Airport in April 1990   **Matthias Hiekel via Bundesarchiv**

Interflug in advertising and popular culture

The most 'popular' exposure of Interflug in popular culture was an eight-episode TV series called Treffpunkt Flughafen (Meeting Point Airport). A co-operation with Cuba's state TV company, the series was shot and broadcast in 1985 and 1986. It accompanies an Ilyushin Il-62 crew led by Captain Werner Steinitz (played by an actor, like all the other protagonists). The cockpit crew of four and their three female flight attendants experience different adventures abroad – part of the series were shot in the Soviet Union, Cuba and Vietnam, with plenty of typical soap opera-esque personal dramas and ups and downs en route. With so much shooting abroad, being in the cast represented something of a jackpot in a society where travel was problematic even for the most politically reliable, let alone flighty creatives.

In episode 1, First Officer Paul Mittelstedt has to pass his final exam, conducted by experienced training captain Werner Steinitz, who is also a good friend. Before his all-important check ride, Paul spends a few days in his home village to celebrate his father's birthday, accompanied by a Cuban friend from university, Santiago. But what a shock: during his absence, preparing for his exams, his fiancée has fallen in love with another man and breaks up with him. Traumatised, he almost fails his check ride, leading to tension with his check captain. In true soap opera style, he passes his typerating in the end and the two become friends again.

In episode 2, the Il-62 crew find themselves stuck in Havana after a lightning strike. The return flight to Berlin is delayed because of thorough technical checks that need to be done. Time for First Officer Paul to visit his old friend Santiago (we met him in episode 1) in his fishing village of Cojimar. Unfortunately, poor Santiago gets delayed because of a cyclone. Paul is fascinated by Paolina, the fiancée of Santiago, a cheerful Cuban girl. The heat of the night, the music... When Santiago comes home and finds out, he is not amused and the two men end up in an almost deadly fight over Paolina.

Episode 3 sees a birdstrike on a flight to Angola carrying morphine and medical equipment and after an emergency landing, hothead First Officer Paul once more gambles not only with his own wellbeing but also that of his fellow crewmembers, negotiating with the local authorities over totally exaggerated airport fees. Weapon dealers find the morphine on board highly interesting. Fortunately, Captain Steinitz calls upon his skills as a diplomat to to salvage the situation and get everybody out alive.

In episode 4, Karin, the sister of co-pilot Paul Mittelstedt, is also part of the crew. She is divorced, has a daughter and struggles to reconcile her strenuous daily work as chief stewardess and the frequent absence from home with her duties as a mother. After a particularly gruelling flight, loneliness and desperation drive her back into the arms of her ex-husband Lutz, from whom she separated mainly because of his women's stories. They spend the night together and that gives Lutz hope for a new beginning. But Karin remains consistent. Even Paul, who liked his brother-in-law, cannot change her mind. And someone else tries to win the heart of the attractive chief stewardess. On her travels Karin meets the quite reserved zoologist Arthur Gerlach. The two get closer during a weather-related forced stay. Gerlach's timid efforts are crowned by little success until the animal expert is called for help when a tropical snake threatens Karin's life.

Episode 5: Commander Werner Steinitz has promised to finally celebrate the birthday of his wife Marion with a short holiday together and books a romantic room in a hotel by the Baltic Sea for the purpose. But as so often in their many years of marriage, Interflug knows no mercy and a special mission puts their plans to shambles: Steinitz has to fly equipment to Angola. He asks his severely disappointed wife to drive up alone and have a good time. Steinitz still hopes that the matter can be settled in no time and that he can at least be there for his birthday to make up for the missed opportunity. But then everything and everybody seems to be conspiring against him. The return flight is delayed by several days. While the long-serving husband is plagued by a guilty conscience, attractive stewardess Viola, who is madly in love with her boss, tries to seduce Steinitz. Meanwhile, during her lonely vacation, to which she finally took her grandson instead of the husband, Mrs. Steinitz meets an understanding gentleman who even proposes to marry her.

Stewardess Li is having a hard time in episode 6 with her jealous fiancé, Hanh. He demands that she give up her work and stay at home. After a visit of her colleagues at Li's parents' house, her relationship with Hanh seems to break up for good. Li has to leave again without having spoken to Hanh again. Paul Mittelstedt, the charming and daredevil copilot, stands by Li's side in this difficult situation like a brother and tries to comfort her. During his next stay in Hanoi he meets Hanh for a discussion between men, trying to put in a good word for Li. Paul doesn't seem to succeed on his mission, because he hurts Hanh's sense of honour with his boyish manner. For himself, on the relationship front, things are also not easy after a breakup from his fiancée. Paul's attempt to land with Caroline Drechsler, the English teacher at the company academy, fails miserably as she is not available for a short adventure.

The last two episodes of the series see our crew in Nicaragua to fly wounded Sandinists to the GDR for treatment and come with all the ingredients of a good soap opera. The end, of course, is a happy one for all involved. The TV series was a major success in the GDR, as would have been the case in countries that did not restrict the movement of their citizens. People were not as well-travelled as they are today and a good old love story set in exotic locations was a winning formula everywhere. It's available today on DVD and YouTube (alas without English subtitles). At least non-German speakers can enjoy some really nice footage of Interflug's fleet.

During the golden age of the 1960s, 1970s and 1980s, many airlines around the world published a wide range of products with their logo on them, be it playing cards, pocket calendars, matches, stickers, luggage tags, pennants, posters, postcards or other giveaways; Interflug was no exception. An almost endless collection of lovingly-designed pieces were created by Interflug's advertising department and many are excellent examples of contemporary design. In addition to pieces published by the airline itself, Interflug's aircraft were also printed on GDR stamps and the Il-62 had at least one brief appearance in The Sandman, a popular children's TV series broadcast in Germany to this day. Yes, the Sandman flew Interflug, too!

Very noteworthy are the first day covers published for many different occasions: inaugural flights all got their own individual first day cover, an envelope with the Interflug logo, often an aircraft and little displays of local art from the new route's destination. Other occasions, like major sports events or the opening of Schönefeld's new passenger terminal, were also frequently celebrated and remembered on these beautiful envelopes.

Another less spectacular TV series of seven episodes, Flugstaffel Meinecke ("Meinecke Flying Squadron") accompanies an agricultural flying squad, a much less visible division of Interflug under normal circumstances. Here once more the everyday business of flying gets mixed with personal drama – marriage problems, friendships put to the test, people falling in and out of love. Flugstaffel Meinecke was first broadcast in 1990, just before the end of the GDR, and all episodes are freely available on YouTube.

This ex French Air Force Se210 Caravelle, F-RAFG, was painted in fantasy Interflug colours for a film and is seen here at Paris Le Bourget in 1981
Jacques Guillem
Previous page: Even kids TV puppet loved to fly Interflug

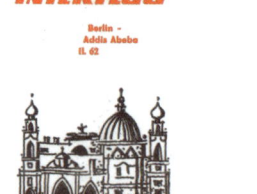

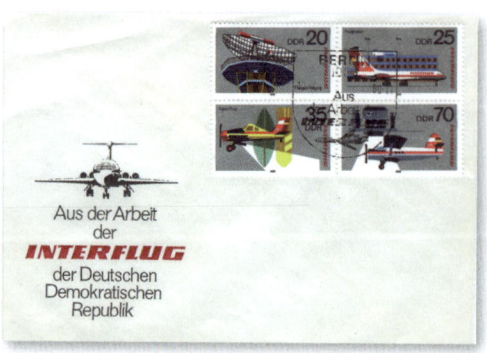

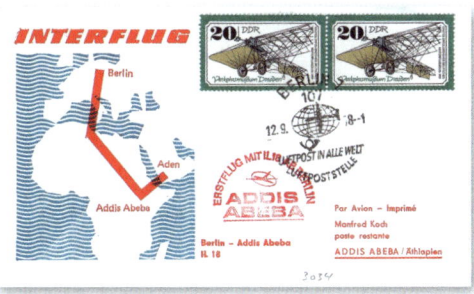

IF
Five in one

The impression may arise that Interflug was only a commercial passenger airline that sometimes flew cargo or government missions. Incorrect! The truth is that Interflug was the name for five different branches: the commercial passenger airline (Verkehrsflug), agricultural flying and remote sensing (Agrarflug), research and industrial flying (Forschungsflug und Industrieflug), airport operations (Betrieb Flughäfen) and air traffic control (Flugsicherung). Until the late 1970s, all five units had distinctive names and even logos.

In 1979, all units were amalgamated under the Interflug brand, with the name of their subdivision added, e.g. Interflug Agrarflug. The distinctive names and logos largely disappeared and henceforth, all used the Interflug name and logo. A smart way to distinguish them were different colours. The commercial airline kept the bright red it had already been using for years, airports were given a light blue, air traffic control got orange, the agricultural unit green and research and industrial flying dark blue.

Let's have a look at the two other flying units of Interflug, the agricultural, and research and industrial flying units. Both existed for the almost the entire history of the airline, and contributed hugely to the development of the GDR. Largely confined to operations within the national borders, they did not play the flag carrier or ambassadorial role of the passenger airline.

The agricultural unit (Agrarflug) was definitely the busiest unit of Interflug in terms of the number of landings and take-offs. Flights typically only lasted a few minutes but often involved dozens and dozens of landings and take-offs each day, from mid-February to the end of October. Agrarflug was of crucial importance to the GDR's agricultural sector.

While mostly busy spreading fertiliser over the fields, the little yellow planes were also used for special missions. In wet years they helped with wheat sowing in autumn, replacing tractors that would have sunk into the soaked field.

But there were also 'out of the box' missions, such as flying children with whooping cough at an altitude of 3,000 meters, which brought them relief; dropping leaflets at festivals and public events; or towing banners.

Agricultural flying dated back to the very early days of Interflug. The first spraying mission took off in March 1957 with a Czechoslovakia-built Aero L-60 Brigadýr. Soon, there were dozens of aircraft operating from bases all over the GDR. Although it was not perfect for the job, the L-60 was an aircraft that was readily available and over the years, the fleet grew to more than 60.

31 were lost in accidents, illustrating the dangerous nature of much

The indestructible An-2 played a big role in developing the GDR's agriculture
Interflug Abteilung Werbung
Previous page: Mi-8 DM-SPA removing snow from roofs in Neubrandenburg
Benno Bartocha via Bundesarchiv

of the flying. The working altitude on flights fighting the potato beetle was only three meters (10 feet) above the ground. Narrow turns were flown at 40 to 50 meters (130 to 160 feet) and at a bank angle of 30 to 40 degrees. Anybody who has seen agricultural aircraft at work knows what a special and challenging type of flying it is. In the L-60, things were very basic and the pilot was sitting right in front of a container of poison that was sprayed onto the fields. When everything was not loaded and closed super carefully, droplets would end up on the clothes or hair. Not nice!

Among the pilots flying it, the L-60 was regarded as a 'widowmaker'. Several pilots lost their life on missions over the years but it took some time until the fleet was replaced by safer, more capable aircraft better up to the job, like the good old Antonov An-2 (which was flown by two pilots, not one) or the newly-developed Let Z-37 Čmelák (Czech for 'bumble bee'), an aircraft developed just for agricultural flying. The introduction of new and better types also increased the safety and operational record of these flights. No matter the danger, the pilots and ground crews never received the same level of glamour and status as their colleagues flying the big iron for Interflug.

With the introduction of the Čmelák, agricultural flying became commonplace in the GDR and there were dedicated airfields (or airfields mostly used for this purpose) in all corners of the country, some of them with their own maintenance bases. A very important airfield was in Kyritz, where a small but fine museum is today dedicated to agricultural flying in the GDR (www.agrarflug-kyritz.de).

The system was organized in different squadrons (copying structures from the military) covering the various regions of the country. Dedicated aircraft like the Z-37 Čmelák, the PZL-106 Kruk (Polish for 'raven') or, later, the PZL-Mielec M-18 Dromader (Polish for 'dromedary') were all operated in large numbers, wore the Interflug insignia, and contributed significantly to the development of agriculture in the GDR.

Spray flights were an elementary part of the successful agriculture enterprise of the GDR, but when the GDR ended, the whole sector was restructured and as was the case so often, things that worked quite well no longer seemed viable, efficient or necessary when seen through

West German or capitalist glasses. Like so many factories or businesses in the GDR, the agricultural unit more or less closed overnight and the amount of flights operated almost fell to zero. The circumstances of the liquidation of this unit remain dubious to this day as with so many transactions that happened in the vacuum after the fall of the Iron Curtain. Most of the agricultural fleet was sold to the United States (the PZL-106s), others to Spain, Canada, and even Australia.

Some local would-be entrepreneurs tried to pick up small remains of this large unit and continue its legacy in the new, capitalist world. Most were not successful in the longer term. Whatever agricultural flying is needed today is often done by helicopters and bigger operators. A few of the yellow aircraft are still flying today, some soldiering on in their role as agricultural aircraft, or were purchased by private owners, and sometimes still wear their original bright yellow colours like the very fine PZL-106 registered D-FOAB, owned by Dieter Gehling from Stadtlohn in far western Germany close to the Dutch border, often appearing at airshows or other aviation events.

Another interesting unit, which interestingly survived the end of Interflug, was for industrial and research flying, which started flying as a subdivision of Interflug's agricultural unit with a pair of Mil Mi-4 helicopters transferred from the National People's Army in 1959, registered DM-SPA and DM-SPB. Their first missions were radio measurement and geophysical reconnaissance flights. During a major cycling event, one of them was used as

The Let-410 was mostly used for remote sensing and aerial photography missions
Interflug Abteilung Werbung

a relay station for the GDR's broadcasting service Deutscher Fernsehfunk. In 1961, the first construction site flights took place, craning heavy pieces into place, an activity that was significantly expanded when the first Mi-8 was delivered in 1967, which could carry three times the weight as the smaller Mi-4.

This unit was formally spun off in 1978, and in 1984 was given its new and final name, FIF, Fernerkundung, Industrie und Forschungsflug (Remote sensing, industrial, and research flight). The helicopter fleet was joined by the first fixed wing aircraft, Antonov An-2s and later, Let-410s. For many years, the electrification of the GDR's railway network and aerial photography were the two main tasks of the unit.

After the end of the GDR, when all the state-owned enterprises of the GDR were to be privatised, the opinion of the Treuhand (the state agency established to oversee privatisation) was that it would be best to 'unwind' Interflug's three flying units (passenger airline, agricultural, and FIF) separately. Prior to being put up for sale, FIF became Berliner Spezialflug (BSF), with 315 employees. Six Let-410s, three An-2s, and the helicopter fleet of Mi-8s were all transferred onto the civil German register. The company was doing quite well financially and even turned a profit in 1991, which avoided a liquidation.

Instead, the company was put up for sale and in August 1991, the German general representative of US aircraft manufacturer Piper won the bid and purchased Berliner Spezialflug for a very reasonable 1 German Mark. In 1991, BSF was even listed on the stock exchange.

Crane flying and aerial photography continued playing a role and its fleet of Let-410s was supplemented by Beech 1900Ds for a brief foray into scheduled passenger flying. While the company headquarters and helicopter base was at Berlin's Schönefeld Airport, passenger flights operated from the more central Tempelhof Airport. The first route was to the German city of Braunschweig. Kassel and Erfurt were two other German

Z-37 Čmelák in action on a crop spraying sortie
Interflug Abteilung Werbung

The remote sensing, industrial, and research flight department later became Berliner Spezialflug. It operated a small fleet of Let-410s on domestic and regional flights, like this one here, D-COXE, seen at Berlin Tempelhof Airport
Ralf Manteufel

Berliner Spezialflug Mil-Mi 8 D-HOXQ on a very special mission, lifting a flight simulator to the top floor of the Europa Center
Luftfahrtarchiv Matthias Winkler

cities soon added. International flights followed, from Tempelhof to Prague, Linz in Austria and the Gothenburg in Sweden, but the experiment did not last long. All fixed wing aircraft were sold or returned to their lessors, and only helicopter flying survives.

Today called Spezialflug Berlin, the company still offers Mi-8s for special missions, and charters aircraft for cargo or passenger flights from other airlines on request. While it still exists and is one of the very few Interflug units that has survived, one can definitely say that Spezialflug is only a shadow of what this quite proud and successful unit of Interflug once was.

The other two units of Interflug were non-flying: air traffic control, and the country's passenger airports. ATC was merged into what later became Deutsche Flugsicherung (DFS), and the GDR's airports were transformed into or joined with existing entities such as Mitteldeutsche Airport Holding (which operates the airports in Dresden and Leipzig) or Flughafen Berlin Brandenburg.

Interflug, Interhotel, Intershop

After the construction of the Berlin Wall in 1961, one prefix became very popular in the GDR: Inter. Interflug was one example, but not the only one. The other two examples were Intershop and Interhotel. Their names promised luxury and internationality, at least at first sight, in a country that was quite isolated and not very international at all.

And when Interhotel or Intershop were established, it really wasn't about being anything, their function was to simply generate much-needed foreign currency for the country. Interhotel was founded in 1965 and operated as a hotel chain, much like the Intourist Hotels in the Soviet Union. The chain originally consisted of one hotel each in Berlin, Erfurt, Jena and Magdeburg, two hotels in Karl-Marx-Stadt (today Chemnitz), and five hotels in the important trade fair city of Leipzig, which saw many international visitors.

Five star properties in the portfolio were almost exclusively open to visitors from the 'non-socialist economic area', and payments had to be made in freely convertible currencies. These included the Interhotel Potsdam, the Metropol and Palasthotel in Berlin, the Merkur in Leipzig or the Bellevue in Dresden.

Four star establishments often hosted guests from the FDGB (Free German Trade Union Federation) and from fraternal nations. A well-known example was Hotel Stadt Berlin (today a Park Inn flagship property), primarily used by guests from the Soviet Union. The lowest category of Interhotels were the three-star facilities, mostly in smaller towns, such as the Hotel Elephant in Weimar. By international standards, the Interhotels were, with some exceptions, probably rated about one star too high.

The chain peaked at 35 Interhotels across the GDR. Half a dozen were exclusively for foreign guests and known as Valuta hotels (Valuta, the Latin word for value, is an international word for hard currency). One was the Merkur in Leipzig, which was extremely lucrative during trade fairs for both the state and for those women who 'captured' businessmen with strong currencies. Prostitution was officially banned since 1968, but with the opening of new Interhotels in the early 1970s, the Stasi deliberately used women and men – 'between 20 and 30 years of age, unmarried, no children, knowledge of foreign languages, good-looking, educated, analytical skills, patriotic sentiments' (as per the official Stasi job description) – to obtain information from and about foreign visitors.

The last Interhotels built include the Hotel Dresdner Hof (opened in 1990, becoming the Dresden Hilton in 1992) and the Domhotel on Berlin's Gendarmenmarkt (also a Hilton today).

The Interhotels were little islands in a country whose population often suffered

An Intershop at Berlin's Friedrichstrasse railway station
KyleJeanMichelle / Wikimedia Commons
Previous page: An Intershop closed for business in Dreden in summer 1990
Ncarste / Wikimedia Commons

from shortages. Almost anything was available there, be it fine food or luxury goods (often sold at the Intershop in the lobby) for foreign currency, and a comfort level largely unknown outside the hotel.

After the German reunification, most Interhotels were temporarily managed by the infamous Treuhand and converted into the Interhotel AG. The majority of them were eventually sold on to private investors and today operated by international chains like Westin or Radisson. Often, their exterior remains a fine example of the brutalist late-period GDR architecture although the interiors have long been sanitised.

Another way for the state to raise hard currency was via the Intershop retail chain. In the early days, they were the mostly to be found in the lobby of Interhotels, which made sense as this was the natural habitat of foreigners with hard currency to spend, and were first called Transitlager (literally 'Transit Camp'), then International Bazaar (or was it actually Internationaler Basar?) before settling on the catchy and brand-aligned Intershop.

Thus until the early 1980s, Intershops were mainly found in Interhotels, at border crossings, at rest areas along transit corridors to Berlin, or at major railway stations.

The shops became a hit (and the government liked the revenues) and their number grew to 470 by 1989, spread all over the country. The highest concentration was found in East Berlin, 20, followed by Rostock, Leipzig and Dresden.

In 1974, GDR citizens were allowed to shop in the Intershops with West German Marks for the first time. But not for long. In 1979, a sharp restriction was implemented: shopping would henceforth only be permitted with forum cheques, an East German unit of currency for holders of hard currency to convert into, to spend locally. Bad for the citizens, good for the government, as the state got a hold on the foreign cash even before its owners even spent it. Only visitors from foreign countries were (of course) still allowed to continue paying with hard currency, including (West-) German Marks, US Dollars, or Austrian Schillings. By the late 1980s, Intershops generated more than a billion German Marks in revenue per year and were a very important contributor to the GDR household.

They sold basically anything that was impossible to get or only available in far inferior quality in regular shops (which were called Konsum): soap, jeans, coffee, chocolate, perfumes, LP records, cassette recorders, glossy magazines. Even larger appliances such as washing machines or refrigerators could be ordered.

What made the Intershops attractive for customers from the West instead of simply buying at home were the low low prices. One reason was that the GDR did not have to pay value added tax on purchases of goods from the Federal Republic. In addition, many of the goods on offer came from local production under license ('Gestattungsproduktion'). During the late years of the GDR, more and more Western companies had their products manufactured cheaply in the GDR, a low-wage country yet able to achieve high quality manufacturing standards when it put its mind to it. In return, they made some of this output available locally in the GDR (albeit not to the average citizen). That included GDR-made cigarettes, chocolate, underwear or coffee.

The money generated by the Intershops was so important that they opened every day of the year, even on holidays. They were a fine example of the economic necessities winning over political or ideological principles. The money to be made was too good to not make it. In 1977, Erich Honecker couldn't have put it better when he said, "These shops are, of course, not a constant companion of socialism. But we can't ignore the fact that the large number of visitors is bringing in much more foreign currency than was previously the case. About 9.5 million guests from capitalist countries come to us every year, who eat with us, stay overnight for the most part, and of course have money in their pockets. Through the Intershops we have created the possibility that this foreign currency stays with us in the country." Without important generators of hard currency like Interhotel, Intershop, or Interflug, the GDR would probably have been in an even more desolate economic condition and at a much earlier stage. After the fall of the Berlin Wall, Intershop's raison d'être no longer existed and the shops were liquidated. Although they no longer exist, the brand is still used today by Intershop Communications, a company offering e-commerce solutions based in Jena in the former GDR.

The gigantic Interhotel Stadt Berlin (today the Park Inn) going up on Berlin's Alexanderplatz
Jörg Blobelt / Wikimedia Commons

Interflug's darkest days

Notlandung
emergency

The darkest day in the 33-year history of Interflug, except maybe for the airline's closure, was without doubt August 14, 1972. The airline's first Ilyushin Il-62, DM-SEA, had been delivered to Schönefeld on Lenin's 100th birthday, April 22, 1970, and entered service days later on the important route to Moscow. Two years later, the big bird was assigned to carry 148 holidaymakers to Burgas Airport in Bulgaria with a crew of eight – four in the back and four up front, headed by Commander Heinz Pfaff. The jet took off from Schönefeld at 16:29.

At 16:43, passing the city of Cottbus 100 kilometers (62 miles) from Berlin and passing through 8,900 metres (29,200 feet), the flight crew noticed problems with the aircraft trim. The return to Schönefeld Airport was initiated and at 16:51 the crew started to dump fuel to avoid an overweight landing. The situation deterorated as cabin crew reported smoke in the rear cabin, and at 16:59 the flight reported control problems.

A hot air pipe in the rear cargo hold had been leaking since they left the gate, damaging the insulation on electrical cables. This led to sparking short circuits which started a fire, intensified upon contact with flammable de-icing fluid. With no fire detection in the rear fuselage, the cockpit crew were unaware of the severity of their troubles (although the truth will have no doubt been dawning on the cabin crew working the aft cabin, and many of their charges too). With pitch control lost, the flight declared an emergency at 16:59, but despite Schönefeld being in sight, it was too late. The rear fuselage separated; absent the downforce of the stabiliser, the big jet pitched down beyond the vertical and hit the ground close to the city of Königs Wusterhausen at 17:00.

While investigations were going on, Interflug's remaining Il-62s stayed on the ground. As a result of the findings, the aircraft received several modifications, including the installation of additional fire detectors and a viewing window in the rear partition. This accident was the worst in Interflug's history, and remains the worst aviation accident on German soil, with 156 lives lost.

On September 1, 1975, Tupolev Tu-134 DM-SCD operated a charter flight from Stuttgart in West-Germany to Leipzig, bringing visitors from West-Germany to the Leipzig trade fair. Shortly before 08:00 in the morning, the aircraft was on final approach in dense fog. The pilots carried out a precision approach, with an air traffic controller monitoring the approach by radar. It was the air traffic controller's task to communicate any necessary corrections to the approach course and altitude to the crew down to a decision height of 60 metres (196 feet). No visual contact with the runway nor even the approach lights by the flight crew at this point necessitated a go-around.

The captain, however, continued the approach and dropped below the safety altitude, flying blind. Neither the co-pilot, the navigator nor the air traffic controller intervened. A kilometre (0.62 miles) short of the runway threshold, DM-SCD collided with the transmitting mast of a radio beacon, damaging the left wing then tearing engine number one from the left rear fuselage. Tu-134 rolled savagely to the left and crashed inverted into the ground. Due to the force of the impact, the aircraft was launched back into the air and did a complete rollover while covering 200 to 250 meters before hitting the the ground again. After a third rollover, in which the Tu-134 broke into three parts, the wreck came to rest 400 metres past the first point of contact and burst into flame. 27 of the 34 people on board lost their lives. Four passengers and the cockpit crew of three survived.

March 26, 1979 saw the only serious accident of an Interflug aircraft outside the GDR. At the time, the Movimento Popular de Libertação de Angola (MPLA), which ruled the socialist brother nation of Angola since its independence, supported the independence movement Zimbabwe African People's Union (ZAPU) operating in Rhodesia, who required heavy weapons for a planned offensive in 1979, which were delivered from the GDR to the Angolan capital Luanda. From there, they were to be flown to Lusaka. As Angolan airline TAAG did not have enough capacity, the purchase of the weapons from the GDR came with an Interflug Il-18 freighter, DM-STL, to deliver this sensitive cargo.

Passenger seats after the crash of Il-62 DM-SEA on 14 August 1972   Bundesarchiv

Cockpit section of the crashed Il-62 DDR-SEW Luftfahrtarchiv Matthias Winkler

This being quite a political mission, there was quite a bit of pressure to make this operation a success. Crew and technicians were temporarily stationed in Luanda and on March 26, DM-STL was about to take off weighing 60.5 tons. V1 is the speed at which there is not enough runway remaining to safely stop in the event of an aborted takeoff, and at the point engine number 2 failed, 56 seconds after brakes release, V1 had passed and safe flying speed was virtually attained. Despite guaranteeing a runway overrun, the captain aborted the take-off.

After leaving the paved surface at high speed, DM-STL collided with some navigation installations and caught fire. The crew of four was killed, as well as six ZAPU members who accompanied the transport, and the aircraft was completely destroyed. Due to the difficult cargo, the circumstances of the accident were kept secret initially. However, as Angola was an ICAO member, an investigation report had to be published, in which food and relief supplies were listed as cargo.

As there were still weapons left to be shipped to Lusaka, a replacement aircraft, Il-18 DM-STP, arrived in Luanda a few days later to carry out the remaining flights. This accident shows how Interflug was sometimes instrumental for political missions, in this case with fatal consequences.

Another accident involving an Il-62 occured towards the end of the GDR (and Interflug), on June 17, 1989. Flight IF102 was operated that day on the trunk route from Schönefeld to Moscow by Il-62M DDR-SEW, only about a year old at the time, with 103 passengers and a flight crew of ten onboard.

When the aircraft reached its take-off speed, the pilots realised that the aircraft's elevator was blocked. With no way of getting the nose up to leave

UP-i6208, originally DDR-SEY, ended its career flying in Iran in 2009, still sporting an Interflug cheatline. It is seen here on the ramp at Tehran's downtown Mehrabad airport just days before it crashed in Mashhad operating Aria Air flight IRX 1525
Guy van Herbruggen

the ground, there was no choice but to abort at high speed. Compounding the situation, instead of cutting the engines to idle and then the outer engines to reverse thrust, the flight engineer accidentally shut down all engines. With no reverse thrust and systems tied to engine-mounted electrical generators winding down, the aircraft glided down the rest of the runway and collided with navigational instruments, some trees and a water tank. When coming to a standstill, the Ilyushin broke apart and caught fire. Luckily, most of the passengers and crew were able to leave the aircraft, although some 15 died during the accident and another six on their way to the hospital or in the hospital at a later stage, and an airport maintenance worker was also injured.

The disaster was on the anniversary of the 1953 East German Uprising and was in the midst of the political crisis that would doom the GDR only months later; rescuers and medical teams were partly held back by the authorities who feared sabotage at work. As so often, a chain of events led to the accident: the actual cause was a faulty design of the elevator which allowed a locking tab to be left in place after routine maintenance; and an appropriate reaction by the flight engineer to the crisis could probably have avoided the runway excursion.

Interflug's final year included a spectacular and thankfully non-lethal swansong in the skies over Moscow on February 11, 1991. At 470 metres (1,550 feet) on approach, the Airbus A310 was given a go-around by air traffic control, which was flown coupled with the autopilot. The captain was uncomfortable or disorientated by the pitch up commanded by the autoflight systems, and pushed forward on his flight controls.

Normally a positive control input would disconnect the autopilot, handing control back to the handling pilot, but this disconnect function is inhibited in go-around mode. Thus the automation attempted to maintain the positive climb profile using the only method remaining at its disposal, stabiliser trim. The trim wheel moved until the stabiliser was in the fully nose up position.

Once the aircraft climbed to its preselected level-off altitude, go-around protections were lost and the autopilot disconnected. Wildly out of trim, the nose reared up to 88 degrees with airspeed dropping through the stall speed to just 30 knots. After shooting up to 1,340 metres (4,400 feet), the aircraft stalled and dropped like a stone with a nose down attitude of 42 degrees, recovered at an altitude of 450 metres (1,476 feet), but with the stabiliser still stuck in the nose up position, the cycle repeated three more times, the final excursion topping out at a dizzying 3,583 metres (11,755 feet). The aircraft was brought under control at 2,650 metres (8,700 feet) and made a safe landing at Sheremetyevo.

The clash of automation and pilot input on go-arounds on Airbus A300-600Rs and A310s claimed many lives in crashes identical to the Interflug incident, notably two identical A300 crashes to befall Taiwanese flag carrier China Air Lines, and a Thai Airways A310 in Surat Thani. Luckily Interflug's final year of operation was not marred by a similar tragedy in Moscow.

There were a number of attempts to hijack Interflug airliners as a means to escape the GDR, however none were successful. The most notorious took place on December 20, 1980. A Tu-134 flying from Berlin to Budapest was the subject of a bomb threat, that a device had been planted onboard with a barometric fuse that would detonate the bomb if the flight descended below 600 metres (1,968 feet), a plot line in common with the 1966 movie The Doomsday Flight. In that Rod Serling-penned thriller, the flight landed at mile-high Denver; on that wintery day over Europe, the Interflug jet headed for Poprad in the mountains of Czechoslovakia (today Slovakia), elevation 718 metres (2,356 feet). After the aircraft was evacuated, a backpack that did not belong to any of the passengers was found; its contents were never disclosed by the authorities.

Luckily D-AOAC's loss of control event over Moscow ended with a safe landing
Interflug Abteilung Werbung

Airbus A310:
Interflug's only widebody

The 1980s were not an easy time for Interflug. The backbone of its fleet was the Tu-134, the Il-18 and the Il-62. All three were noisy, smoky and thirsty aircraft, the latter trait not only a moral failing but also hitting Interflug's bottom line compared to its Western equivalents. The Tu-134 in particular did not meet the noise regulations coming into force at many European airports, yet it was the only aircraft type really suited to these routes in terms of size. And most of Interflug's aircraft were approaching the end of their life and either in need of replacement or for major overhauls, done in the USSR and taking the aircraft out of service for up to six months, compared to a matter of weeks, even for major maintenance events, in Western countries. More modern and efficient Soviet-built replacement aircraft like the Tu-204 or Il-96 were also delayed or dealing with technical difficulties. Buying in the West was out of the question – until exactly that happened!

The A310 was the second product to come from Airbus, which had formed in 1970 to share the talent and resources of European aerospace companies. Separately, they had created a number of technologically innovative designs, but even the successful ones had been produced in relatively small numbers, and some, such as the Vickers VC-10 (54 built), the VFW-Fokker 614 (19 built), the Aerospatiale/BAC Concorde (20 built, 14 sold), and the Dassault Mercure (11 built), had been commercial disasters. The first fruits of this pan-European enterprise was the A300, the world's first twin-engine widebody, intended for heavily-patronised short and medium haul trunk routes. With room for over 300 passengers plus 22 LD3 containers in the belly, it was a workhorse that was popular with passengers and airline accountants alike. After a slow start, the A300 made it to 561 sales, with production lasting from 1971 until 2007.

Airbus aspired to creating a whole family of airliners, and the second machine in their portfolio was the A310, 7.5 metres shorter than the A300, with a smaller wing area, longer range, and a two-person digital cockpit. The A310 was intended as a 707 and DC-8 replacement, and found its main niche as a boutique widebody airliner for smaller carriers that lacked the traffic flows that could fill the considerably larger Ilyushin Il-86 or American jumbos (the 747, L-1011, DC-10), all of which were optimised for over 300 passengers.

Through the mediation of the Bavarian Prime Minister (and Chairman of the Airbus Supervisory Board) Franz Josef Strauss, an almost revolutionary business came about: following lengthy discussions and negotiations, in June 1988, a contract was signed between Interflug and Airbus over the purchase of three factory-new

Airbus A310-304s, Interflug's first Western-built aircraft and the only widebody the airline was ever to operate.

Financing was assured through Western banks and the deal had to be approved by CoCom, the Coordinating Committee on Multilateral Export Controls, a body controlling the exports of Western technology to countries of the Eastern Bloc. And it was: as manufacturer Boeing was close to a deal with Polish airline LOT over the delivery of six Boeing 767s, the US-influenced body could not agree to one deal and refuse to accept the other. As well as a huge leap in productivity and efficiency for Interflug, a deal for Airbus widebodies was also a step towards legitimacy and global recognition the GDR sought even in what transpired to be its last days.

Prior to delivery, additional fuel tanks were installed in the three Airbuses so that non-stop flights to Cuba, Japan or Singapore became possible, increasing the range to 10,430 kilometres (6,481 miles) in still air. Although the regular range of the Airbus A310 exceeded anything any of Interflug's Soviet fleet had to offer, Interflug wanted to operate these flights (in particular the ones to Cuba) non-stop, and not only for commercial reasons. Flights on the route to Havana operated by the Il-62 usually stopped in Gander, Newfoundland. And during these stops, GDR citizens managed to apply for asylum there quite frequently, something the GDR leadership was absolutely not happy about. With the delivery of the Airbuses, flights to Cuba would be able to operate without this loophole to asylum.

The aircraft's configuration was very passenger friendly: just 208 seats including 42 in so-called Club Class. The Airbuses featured overhead TV screens and passengers were invited to use an on-board library or Interflug branded fitness bands for their entertainment.

Part of the deal was training of the flight crews with Airbus in France and a maintenance contract with West German Lufthansa, bringing the two carriers closer together even though the German reunification was not predictable or imminent when the contract was signed.

A new addition to the line up at Schoefeld, June 1990
Previous page: the cavernous interior of the A310

Erwin Schneider via Bundesarchiv

A gorgeous study of Interflug's DDR-ABB basking in the high altitude sunshine over a soon-to-be reunited Europe *Interflug Abteilung Werbung*

Only about a year after the ink under the purchase contract was dry, the first of three Airbus A310s, registered DDR-ABA, touched down at Schönefeld Airport from Toulouse on June 26, 1989. It was wearing a new "Eurowhite" colour scheme which retained the iconic Interflug logo on the tail. Apart from a leased Dash 8, which had more of an anecdotal character in the last weeks of Interflug, the Airbuses were the only Interflug aircraft ever wearing this colour scheme.

For the pilots in particular, moving from Russian aircraft usually operated by a cockpit crew of four to the digital cockpit of the Airbus A310 flown by two was a quantum leap. 26 of them were initially sent to Toulouse for conversion training, accompanied by flight attendants and technical staff, who also needed to be trained on the new type. Another contract was signed between Interflug and Lufthansa, for the training of maintenance crews at the maintenance centres in Frankfurt and Munich, and flying instructors onboard Lufthansa flights.

Following a technical proving flight to Russia, which almost became a disaster because of the complete failure of the aircraft's navigation system, the first Airbus entered commercial service flawlessly just a few days later, on July 1st. The inaugural flight was a morning return flight to Athens, followed by an evening service on that same day to Dubai, Bangkok and Singapore, flight number IF 720.

The second Airbus, DDR-ABB, was delivered on June 30, with DDR-ABC bringing up the rear on October 25, 1989. Apart from the route to Dubai, Bangkok and Singapore, the type operated on scheduled flights to Beijing, Havana (a route which was later extended to Mexico), Larnaca, Athens and Rome among others, as well as charter flights. By year-end, the three Airbuses had accumulated 738 flights and 4,238 flight hours. And they were up in the air much more than their counterparts: when the Il-62 fleet averaged just over four flight hours per aircraft per day and the Tu-134 even less, the Airbuses did much better at around 10.5 flight hours per aircraft per day. Suddenly, Interflug's operation got an efficiency boost.

A postcard promoting the new Airbus A310 as Interflug flies into the sunset
Previous page: A310 DDR-ABA taxiing at Schönefeld Airport. In the background, the three Il-62s recently transferred to the German Air Force can be seen
Luftfahrtarchiv Matthias Winkler

When the airline stopped flying and was liquidated in 1991, the three Airbuses were deemed one of the few real assets of the airline, at least as far as its fleet was concerned. They were transferred to the German Air Force, ultimately replacing the Luftwaffe's Boeing 707s. DDR-ABA (later D-AOAA) became 10+21, the official German government aircraft (Germany's "Air Force One"), with sister aircraft 10+22 (ex DDR-ABB/D-AOAB) its replacement. The third A310, DDR-ABC (D-AOAC), became 10+23 and is the only one of the three still in service with the German government.

10+21 and 10+22 were retired from service with the Air Force in 2011 and 2014 respectively and replaced by a pair of two more capable former Lufthansa Airbus A340-300s now flying Germany's politicians around the world. 10+22 ended up in Iran (which caused a bit of embarassment in Germany, as Iran was still under sanctions at that time, before the nuclear treaty to which Germany remains committed to the present day) and briefly flew for Mahan Air as EP-VIP and later EP-MMX. It is allocated for a new Iranian airline, Tehran Airlines, and was apparently registered to them as EP-THR but does not seem to be active as of summer 2020 (and spring 2025).

The other Airbus A310, 10+21, was only released from government service in 2014 and sold to SA Novespace for Zero Gravity flights, where it remains active until this day. The last former Interflug Airbus A310, ex-DDR-ABC / D-AOAC, was still flying for the German Air Force, based at Cologne/Bonn Airport, as 10+23, wearing an all-grey colour scheme, until it was retired in 2021. It was equipped in an all-Economy Class configuration of 214 seats and mostly used for troop transportation. After its retirement, the aircraft was purchased by a theme park in Northern Germany, Serengeti Park Hodenhagen, with plans to convert it into a café inside the park. The last flight of the aircraft took it to Hannover in September 2021 but plans to disassemble and take the aircraft into the park by truck were delayed until 2025 (can you believe it) as some trees were standing on the planned route and fears were raised they could be damaged by the passing truck with the Airbus fuselage loaded on it. After a court trial, the permission was eventually granted and a solution found and hopefully, 10+23 will find a permanent new home inside the park.

Interflug's short-lived Dash 8

Maybe the most unusual aircraft type in Interflug's fleet, definitely the one that spent the shortest time in service was a single De Havilland Dash 8 which operated for just a few months, between late 1990 and spring 1991.

Interflug had previously operated what could be considered a commuter class airliner for regular passenger flights, when Antonov An-24s were operated on domestic and shorter international flights between 1966 and 1975. When domestic flying stopped, the An-24s were retired.

With the German reunification in October 1990 (and already before that), Interflug saw itself in a new environment which prioritised efficiency and profit. With its fleet of aging and fuel-guzzling Tupolev Tu-134s, Ilyushin Il-18s and Il-62s, the airline would not be able to compete on a level playing field. Thus, the search for alternatives began. The Boeing 737 was given sufficiently serious consideration to appear in timetables, but never delivered. A British Aerospace BAe 146, wearing the colours of Air UK, was demonstrated to the airline in the spring of 1990, but Interflug weren't convinced.

It was a personal contact that led to a single Dash 8 wearing Interflug colours, at least for a couple of months. Representatives of Interflug, like most major airlines, regularly attended the IATA slot conference, held twice a year. Over the years, people from the various airlines became familiar faces and drinking buddies, and it was at one of these events that the Interflug delegation asked the team from Austrian regional carrier Tyrolean whether they would consider operating a regional aircraft for some of Interflug's thinner routes. At the time, Tyrolean's Manfred Helldoppler held the title of Manager – Flight Operations Support, and was a regular attendee at the IATA conferences.

Through its Tyrolean Aircraft Leasing subsidiary, the airline had experience leasing oUTaircraft to airlines all over the world. A Dash 8 series 103, registered OE-LLI, was immediately available. Both parties met once in Berlin and once in Vienna, and within a period of just a few weeks, the deal was signed for a wet lease to Interflug. Tyrolean made a good partner in more ways than just airframe availability; Manfred Helldoppler suspects that dealing with an Austrian company was more neutral for Interflug than asking a carrier from the former West Germany for assistance.

With 37 seats, the aircraft seemed to be well-matched to short and thin routes like Berlin to Copenhagen, Prague and Warsaw. Helldoppler remembers that when it came to rostering the aircraft and crews, his Interflug colleagues asked him how many rotations it could possibly operate per day, one or two? One or two roundtrips per day was the typical routine

DHC-8-102 OE-LLI on approach to Schönefeld
Previous page: DHC-8-102 OE-LLI next to a Tu-134 at Schönefeld   Luftfahrtarchiv Matthias Winkler

for a Tu-134 or Il-18, with significant ground time between flights. When the answer was, "At least four," the reaction from his counterpart was complete surprise.

And four daily roundtrips what was the aircraft actually operated once it was delivered to Schönefeld in late October 1990: an early morning roundtrip to Prague, followed by daytime flights out to Warsaw and Copenhagen and back, followed by another evening service to Prague and back, all flown daily.

The Dash 8 wore a livery very similar to the Interflug A310s, which was almost no livery at all: the Interflug logo in the tail, with Interflug titles and a small flag underneath the cockpit windows on an all-white fuselage (a style known as Eurowhite as it was pioneered by UTA French Airlines, many of whose neighbours followed suit by dispensing with cheatlines).

The cockpit crews and mechanics were all Canadians, supplied through Tyrolean's leasing arm; the cabin crews were all Austrians supplied by Tyrolean Airways. While the interiors were not customised, Interflug safety cards were created for the type, quite a rarity among collectors today.

The operation of the Dash 8 went without a hitch; Interflug was positively surprised by the high level of efficiency and reliability, and keen to develop this co-venture further, planning additional international destinations from Berlin, and a proposed triangle route from Leipzig and Dresden to Vienna (which Austrian Airlines later operated for years, using the Dash 8).

A timetable was produced as normal for the usual winter timetable period from late October 1990 until March 30, 1991. In that version, flights to Copenhagen, Prague and Warsaw were operated by EQV, the great tombola in the sky for type collecting aviation enthusiasts, short for 'equipment varies'. In an updated version that was valid from March 30 1991, the Dash 8 actually appeared as aircraft type on these routes.

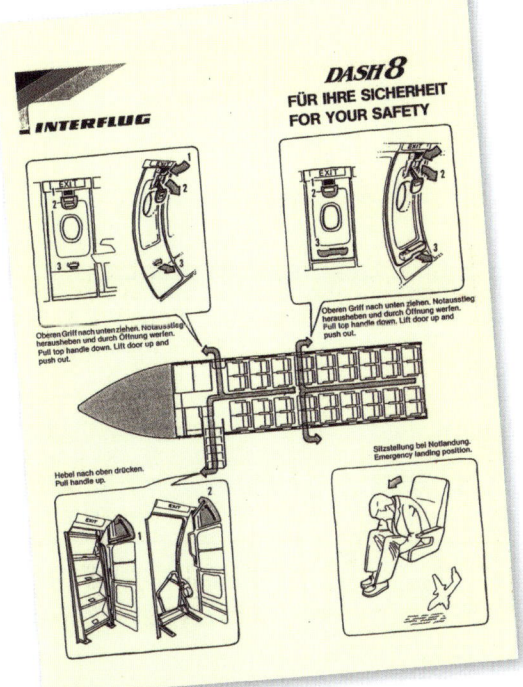

Events overtook these aspirations, with Interflug's last passenger service operating on April 30; the sad honour of the last flight ever operating under an Interflug callsign fell to the humble Dash 8 when it was ferried from Berlin back to its owners in Innsbruck on May 4, using IF 0001 as flight number.

After its short intermezzo with Interflug, OE-LLI had a most interesting life. It operated for Albanian Airlines, Tyrolean, Air Senegal. Perhaps missing its halcyon days in reunification-era Germany, it flew as D-BFRA for Augsburg Airways between 1997 and 2000. It went on to Sunstate Airlines in Australia, Airlines PNG in Papua New Guinea, and Solomon Airlines in the Solomon Islands, about as far as you can go from Austria. In 2017, it was registered in Canada as C-FGCP and today, at 29 years old, it operates for Canadian charter carrier Chrono Aviation in a very cool all-black colour scheme, based in Montréal.

30 years later, the aircraft has found a new home in Canada where it operates with Chrono Aviation.
Brian Tattuinee

Interflug eyewitness reports

Unfortunately I never had the chance to fly Interflug myself as a passenger, so all the knowledge I have is from other people's experiences or published reports. When Interflug stopped flying in 1991, I was just 13 years old. Two of my good friends had a chance to fly Interflug as a passenger several times, proving that the benefit of age is experience.

While many people flew Interflug far more often than these two, both are avid aviation enthusiasts and have worked in the industry themselves for decades.

Theo Handstede is a retired Lufthansa long haul purser. He has thousands of flights in his logbook, many in a professional capacity, and many private trips to places all over the world. As an aircraft and airline collector, he often flies a particular route simply to tick off a particular aircraft type or airline.

His first flight with Interflug was in 1989, on Ilyushin Il-62 DDR-SEU operating flight IF 482 from Berlin Schönefeld to Amsterdam. Interflug had been flying people from the West for decades, so getting from West-Berlin to Schönefeld airport was, if not entirely hassle-free, a fairly straightforward routine.

He took the shuttle bus from West Berlin's central bus station close to the trade fair (where it still is today). Crossing the border in an Interflug bus close to Schönefeld Airport at Waltersdorfer Chaussee usually did not even involve formal border control; a member of the GDR border patrol boarded the bus at the checkpoint and travelled the short distance to Terminal B, the dedicated check-in area for Westerners at Schönefeld Airport, ensuring that no GDR citizen could board the transit bus and thus enter the 'Western area' of the airport unnoticed.

Check-in, passport control, and security checks for passengers originating from West Berlin took place separately; it was only once in the large airside concourse that West met East for the first time. On the ground at Schönefeld, Theo noticed a feeling of being supervised, more so than at other airports. He recalls many mirrors and a feeling that was generally a bit uneasy.

The flight itself, other than being operated by an Il-62, was quite uneventful. Food and beverage service was no different from other airlines. He recalls everything being served on a plastic tray and the dominant colour Interflug red. The beer, served from a big bottle, was delicious! On all his flights, Theo never "outed" himself as a Lufthansa colleague. He knew (also from his own experience when meeting Interflug crew in the crew hotel in Singapore) that they were not supposed to speak to their West German colleagues, thus he did not want to bring them into an awkward situation. Crews were of all ages really and always pleasant and well-groomed, as far as his three

Bordinformation · Flight information

Wie wird das Wetter am Zielflughafen? – Weather at destination

Sonne · Clear	Regen · Rain	Schnee · Snow	Temperatur · Temperature
☀	☂	❄	.16 +°C / –°C

Kapitän · Captain STIEBRITZ	**Weiterflug · Flight continues at** ./.
Flugstrecke · Route BERLIN – AMSTERDAM	**Überflug · Position** OSTSEE
Datum · Date 12. 08. 1984	**Überflug · Position** NORDSEE
Startzeit · Departure 08. 13 Uhr	**Überflug · Position**
Flugzeugtyp · Aircraft TU–134/A DDR–SCV	**Außentemperatur · Outside temperature** –51°C
Flughöhe · Altitude 10. 600 m	**1. Stewardeß · 1. Stewardess** A. LUTZE
Fluggeschwindigkeit · Speed 850 km/h	**Stewardeß · Stewardess** H. ANDREAS
Entfernung · Distance 1290 km	**Stewardeß · Stewardess** K. KAHLISCH
Flugzeit · Total flight time 1. 45 Stunde	**INTERFLUG** DEUTSCHE DEMOKRATISCHE REPUBLIK
Landung · Arrival Ortszeit · Local time in AMSTERDAM : 10.00 Uhr	

An early version of the computerised map displays of today: an information sheet handed around the cabin explaining the technical aspects of the flight. More often than not, it ended up in someone's pocket as a souvenir.

Previous image: The Il-62 was often used for busy European flights

Collection Daniel Frohriep-Ichihara
Interflug Abteilung Werbung

flights were concerned but not particularly outstanding or unusual compared to their colleagues on any other European carrier.

The Amsterdam route demonstrated how Interflug was unable to fly through West German airspace, leading to long detours; thus, on the route to Amsterdam, Interflug flew north out of Berlin via Danish airspace before routing southwest to the Netherlands, adding an hour to a flight time which is today just over an hour in total.

His second flight was just a few weeks later, from Schönefeld to Budapest. This was busy route between two of the biggest Warsaw Pact nations of communist Europe, thus mostly operated by the people-moving Ilyushin Il-18 (DDR-STE had the honours) instead of the smaller Tupolev Tu-134. A short flight allowed Theo to experience the aircraft type without the commitment of a long sector – perfect! His experience on this flight was similar to the Il-62 flight a few weeks earlier.

For these two flights on Interflug, Theo purchased his tickets at a travel agency in Frankfurt which specialised in low fare tickets on the East German airline, before the concept of a low cost airline existed.

Theo's last flight on Interflug was on the sturdy Tu-134. This was in the interesting (and short) period between late 1990 and early 1991 where Lufthansa wet-leased both Interflug Tu-134s and Pan Am Boeing 727s and operated them on their domestic network. During the reunification of Germany, demand for domestic flights to Berlin and other East German cities like Leipzig and Dresden exploded and exceeded what Lufthansa could reasonably have handled with their own aircraft and crews, so you could fly a Pan Am 727 or an Interflug Tu-134 with a Lufthansa flight number, and on a Lufthansa staff ticket, which is what Theo did this time. Glorious days!

This flight took place on September 17, 1990. LH 6020 from Hamburg to Leipzig was operated by Tu-134 DDR-SCN. This time, things were quite different, as it was a Lufthansa flight, so he could travel on a staff ticket, check-in was done by Lufthansa and the inflight product was the standard Lufthansa choice of meals and beverages (even served from a Lufthansa trolley) and even the inflight magazine was Lufthansa's now.

Although the crew was entirely Interflug, service, as far as Theo recalls it, was the typical Lufthansa domestic service with a small meal and beverages. Quite surprisingly, he does not remember even a single eyebrow raised when passengers, most of them from West Germany, were boarding an Interflug aircraft on this Lufthansa service, something that surprised him back then. But then, the flights were published in the Lufthansa timetable as operated by IF, so maybe all passengers studied the timetable well - or simply didn't care?

Arriving into Leipzig Airport, he remembers, the facility was in quite good shape, as it had always been a major entry point into the GDR for international visitors from all over the world coming to Leipzig's trade fair, so national pride ensured that it always taken good care of.

Another friend lucky enough to have flown Interflug as a passenger on three occasions is Luc Bereni. Today he is the CEO of French airline Air Corsica and has collected thousands of interesting flights over the years, even without ever flying as a pilot or cabin crew himself.

His first visit to the GDR was in March 1978 for a football match. Luc is not only an aviation enthusiast but also a passionate supporter of SC Bastia, a football club from his native home Corsica, who played in European competitions at the time including an away match against Carl Zeiss Jena, necessitating a daytrip from Bastia to Erfurt and back aboard a French-built Sud Aviation Caravelle, operated by Air Charter. The match was won by Jena.

Luc's first flight on Interflug was three years later, on September 19, 1981. Once again, he was returning home from a football match in Helsinki, using an IATA ticketing trick, where you could squeeze a number of flights on different airlines into an itinerary, all for the same IATA-set fare, as long as you did not exceed a certain number of of total miles (usually 20% on top of the point-to-point mileage). After flying down from Helsinki to Warsaw, he connected to a LOT Polish Airlines Il-18 to East Berlin, where he stayed overnight at the massive Interhotel Stadt Berlin on Alexanderplatz (today a Park Inn).

The next morning, a lovely autumn day, he set out for Schönefeld in the morning, despite his flight not leaving until evening, as he planned to spend the day on Schönefeld's famous observation deck. Perhaps surprising for countries that supervised their citizens quite strictly, but many of the airports in Warsaw pact countries had nice observation decks (with Prague having perhaps the best one). He spent a lovely few hours on the terrace and remembers that it was here that he thought for the first time, "Maybe this is quite a nice country after all." While the city and hotel felt a bit depressing to him, everybody (the terrace was quite crowded with families) seemed to have a rather good time here, with no sign of Stasi agents or any other form of supervision.

His evening flight was on an Il-18, DDR-STO, to Prague, quite a short hop. It was the only time that Luc departed from the GDR as an East Berlin originating passenger, not as a transit guest from West Berlin, so he used the same check-in counters as the locals. While remembering the same slightly uneasy feeling while undergoing departure formalities that Theo described, the flight itself was extremely pleasant. Prague was one of the shortest international flights in Interflug's route network, and truly spectacular for Luc as an enthusiast, because an Il-18 was not an easy catch, even in their heyday.

Flight number two happened eight years later, in March 1989. Perestroika was already in full swing and the fall of the Berlin Wall was only months away and a change of atmosphere in the country could definitely be felt, he remembers. Luc boarded an Interflug flight from Athens to Schönefeld on an Il-62, the superstar of the fleet, registered DDR-SEF. The Il-62 replaced the smaller Tu-134 on the route during the high season and this time, Luc worked for French airline Air Inter and was able to use the staff travel agreement that was in place with Interflug.

Except for charter flights, Interflug was never a regular guest in Paris, but the airline had a small local office that sold tickets and managed commercial relationships with other airlines, and this is where he went to pick up his ticket. As is the case with most staff travel, this was a standby ticket, so he wanted to make absolutely sure he would get on the flight, and thus chose the first day of Il-62 operations for the season, where the flight might be busy on the outbound leg from Berlin to Athens, but likely to have plenty of empty seats on the way back. His plan worked: the flight was only half full. Luc recalls that most of the passengers seemed to be headed for West Berlin, taking advantage of Interflug's low fares. One of the best thing on Interflug's flights was the "Bordinformation", an information leaflet the crew filled in for every flight. It told passengers all the details about the flight such as the flight date, routing, altitude and speed, temperatures, sometimes the cities that were overflown as well as the names of the crew. These leaflets were supposed to be circulated around the cabin and

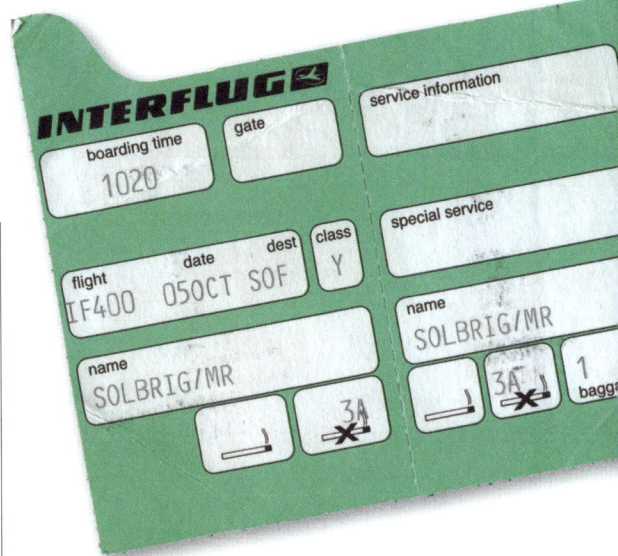

usually ended up in someone's pocket before landing. The meal service, as he remembers it, consisted of a plastic tray with a selection of cold cuts and bread on it.

After landing in Schönefeld, he cleared immigration, hopped on the bus to West Berlin and even had time to catch an evening flight back to France. From touching down at Schönefeld to checking in at Tegel Airport took just over two hours, illustrating that the procedure was very straightforward and the shuttle buses ran frequently.

One thing he remembers from his Interflug flights (and those on other Eastern European carriers) was, in the short period of perhaps a few minutes between "boarding complete" and the first engine starting, the curtain in front of the first row of passenger seats was firmly closed and a few people seemed to come and go. This was probably just the ramp agent or ground staff verifying the loads with the cockpit crew before departure, but to him, this always had a very secretive feel to it.

Luc's last flight on Interflug was, like Theo's, aboard a Tu-134 operating a Lufthansa flight. On March 1, 1991, just a few weeks before Interflug closed shop, he flew from Dresden to Stuttgart, one of many new domestic routes that were opened within just a few weeks of the two Germanies becoming one. LH 6037 was operated by D-AOBO, previously DDR-SDE and originally delivered new to Interflug in September 1975. With German reunification on 3 October 1990, the GDR and also the GDR's aviation registry no longer existed and 17 of Interflug's Tu-134s, seven Il-18s and eleven Il-62 changed onto the now all-German registry as D-AOAD, E, F, G, H, I, J, K, L, M, N for the Il-62s, D-AOAO, P, Q, R, S, T, U for the Il-18s and D-AOBA, C, D all the way until D-AOBS for the Tu-134s. The registration part "D-AO" was only a provisional solution and the "O", this is just speculation on the author's part, could have stood for "Ost" or "East".

When inquiring about the booking figures, this flight appeared to be quite full but in the end, he was easily accommodated aboard a half empty plane. Just like Theo on his Lufthansa service operated by IF, Luc did not notice any surprised looks when passengers boarded the Interflug aircraft even though they had booked a Lufthansa flight.

The service, he remembers, was the standard Lufthansa soft product for the era, drinks served in Lufthansa glasses from a Lufthansa trolley and the seatbag containing the transparent plastic bag with a Lufthansa inflight magazine and sickness bag and an Interflug safety instruction card, what an interesting mix! One thing he remembers vividly was the very poor condition of Dresden Airport, and the novelty of checking in for a flight at a Lufthansa counter and then boarding an Interflug aircraft.

On his three flights, Luc recalls the crew reflecting a bit the change of times: in 1981, the crew to him looked almost "Soviet" in the way they wore their uniform and interacted with passengers. A change could definitely be noticed on his second flight and even more so on the Tu-134 operated Lufthansa flight, things seemed a lot more casual somehow to him.

Luc regrets not flying on one of Interflug's Airbus A310s, but this was a perfect day: two flights on a Lufthansa Boeing 737-200 (Paris-Munich-Dresden), one leg in a Tu-134, and the return home to Paris from Stuttgart on a Lufthansa Boeing 727. Truly flying in style!

The downtown ticket office at Alexanderplatz was the starting point for many journeys with Interflug
Klaus Franke via Bundesarchiv

Experiencing Interflug right after the wall fell

Guest chapter by Andreas Spaeth

Friday December 1, 1989 is a memorable day in German aviation history and deeply engraved in my personal memory. I was a young aviation reporter at the time. The Berlin Wall had fallen very unexpectedly just three weeks prior, and the two Germanys were in a state of flux. Everything was changing quickly. It was undecided if there would be two Germanys in the future, or just one unified nation. Meanwhile, linking the two states was of utmost priority, having been separated for 45 years.

But just establishing new internal flights between the FRG and the GDR wasn't that easy. As the Inner German Border was still a so-called ADIZ (Air Defence Identification Zone), it could not simply be overflown. West Berlin had three allied-controlled air corridors linking it to the rump of West Germany, but there was no such transit facility for air traffic between the two Germanys. On December 1, 1989, two important new air links were established: Lufthansa from Munich to Leipzig, and Interflug from Dresden to Hamburg. I was supposed to take part in both in a single day, starting in Munich, where I was studying at the time, and ending up in Hamburg, where I hail from. Perfect – or so I thought.

The unexpected hurdles initially had no connection to the new thaw between East and West. We took off from the (now long-defunct) Munich Riem airport at 6am aboard a Fokker 50, operated by Lufthansa regional subsidiary DLT. Just after rotation we experienced a bird strike and had to come back for an emergency landing, which went well, while fire trucks and ambulances were lined up.

A spare DLT Fokker 50 was dragooned and we took off again towards what was then Czechoslovakia, as we had to make a major detour to avoid the Inner German Border. About an hour after take off I saw a flight attendant break down crying in the galley, followed by a distressed-sounding announcement from the captain that we had a hydraulics problem, and would have to return to Munich, again. So for the second time in three hours, we came in for an emergency landing at Riem, with other planes diverted and rescue teams lining the runway's edge. All went well, again. A now pale looking station manager seemed extremely relived to see us again, still unharmed.

Many guests and media people had had enough and returned to downtown Munich. Also, there were now no more airworthy aircraft available, with two Fokkers declared AOG (Aircraft On Ground). The hardy travellers who were still committed to fly to Leipzig that day were cheered up by a full bathtub of miniature Veuve Clicquot champagne while waiting for a ride. A Lufthansa Boeing 737-200 that had taken off from Frankfurt to Leipzig was ordered to make an unplanned stop in Munich to pick us up.

But as we finally arrived over Leipzig, actually on the third attempt this morning, the airport was closed due to thick icy fog, or rather, smog, a typical occurrence in the then heavily air-polluted East. As the 737 had more sophisticated navigation systems than most Soviet-built aircraft and there was a mission to fulfil, the pilot decided to land anyway. (In fact the weather was below minima for a Fokker 50, had either of our attempts to fly to Leipzig in one been successful.)

Having landed, the problem was that we couldn't see a thing on the ground as the icy smog was so thick. So much for the photos I was supposed to take of this very exotic location. After a few speeches, a colleague and I were in a rush to get to Dresden to join that evening's inaugural flight to Hamburg.

The way we got to Dresden is my first real eternal memory of Interflug. We were chauffeured the 120 kilometre journey along the bumpy East German autobahn in an official Interflug Lada, grey with Interflug stickers, with Klaus Henkes, Interflug's Director and Lieutenant-General of the East German Nationale Volksarmee (NVA), and driven by his red-haired, flamboyant assistant, Rosemarie Meichsner.

This felt absolutely surreal to me, as only a few months prior I had tried to reach out from West Germany to get any kind of information from Interflug for an article. This was easy with all other Eastern Bloc airlines, but it was impossible to get in touch with Interflug. And now here I sat with the airline president speeding

Passengers boarding the inaugural flight from Dresden to Hamburg both Andreas Spaeth
Previous page: The fashionable 'Eurowhite' livery of the Malev Tu-154 suggests times are changing

Tu-134 DDR-SCX is almost ready to operate the inaugural service from Dresden to Hamburg

Andreas Spaeth

through an exotic country so close, but mentally so far away from the Germany that was my home country.

Dresden, partner city of my hometown Hamburg and also located on the Elbe river, greeted us with sunshine. I will never forget seeing my first Interflug Ilyushin Il-62 gleaming in the winter sun.

After a few speeches, members of the media, an official delegation from Dresden headed by its mayor, some actual passengers, and I boarded our Tupolev Tu-134 of Interflug. Everybody was enthusiastic. We were given small bottles of famous East German Rotkäppchen bubbly, adorned by an Interflug ribbon, a great souvenir.

The friendly captain welcomed me into the cockpit of the first Soviet aircraft I ever flew on. I was amazed by all the gauges, the turquoise colour of the panels, and not least, the transparent nose, made entirely of glass panes.

The passenger cabin was fairly narrow, with just two seat blocks on either side of the aisle. I sat in row 1 facing backwards, with tables dividing the space between us and the facing seats of row 2. We were given a tasty dinner tray with cold cuts and cheese and even tomatoes, which was a surprise, as we were told fresh vegetables were a rare treat in the GDR.

Though we had to fly a detour over the Baltic Sea to avoid the ADIZ and enter West German airspace from Denmark, the flight was swift, about an hour in the air. Before we knew it, we had landed in Hamburg, where it was dark already. As this first airline flight from East Germany to Hamburg was a political event full of symbolism, the mayor of Hamburg and his delegation were lined up at the bottom

Dresden's mayor Wolfgang Berghofer enjoying the inflight service on the inaugural flight to Hamburg
Andreas Spaeth

of the steps to greet the guests of honour from Dresden, led by his mayor colleague.

On board there was some confusion about the protocol, and it was decreed, press out first, so I was one of the first to step down onto the tarmac, I was welcomed profusely as a presumed East German by the mayor of my own hometown, who apparently didn't know about protocol either. Another memorable snippet from an outstanding day.

My next and last Interflug experience came in its final months. It was March 1991, and by now it was clear that the East German airline would not find a role in the new Germany, unified since the previous October. There was a hope that Interflug would succeed, but cash was scarce now that the carrier was exposed to the free market.

Western companies embarked on barter deals. A business travel magazine I freelanced for as a student ran advertising for Interflug, and were given an allocation of flight tickets in return, which ended up not being used, as the publisher was based in Munich, far from Berlin Schönefeld. As the end of Interflug became apparent, the publisher, normally a tight-fisted executive, sent out an internal memo to all staff that anyone could make use of this free ticket allocation on Interflug.

Being a student with little money but very keen for any travel opportunity, especially for free, I took the chance and got myself a round trip in Club Class (Interflug's business class) on one of their new Airbus A310s from Berlin to Bangkok. I flew up to Berlin-Tegel by a former Pan Am Boeing 727, now operated by Lufthansa, then by bus and S-Bahn suburban train for the long journey out to Schönefeld airport, where, late in the evening, my Interflug A310 flight departed.

We flew first to Moscow Sheremetyevo, where a few passengers got off. By now the cabin was mostly empty and I was the only passenger in Club Class, which seated 42 passengers in six rows of 2-3-2 (with the last two rows set aside for smokers). I stretched out as well as I could despite the rather narrow seat pitch. Before landing, I went to the galley to request some breakfast. As on my DLT Fokker, once again I was confronted by weeping flight attendants. When they heard that I was a Western journalist, I found out the cause of their distress as they complained bitterly of being made redundant and robbed of their future very soon. A slightly bizarre and very German moment while we approached over the rice paddies of Thailand in one Interflug's last long haul flights.

The return flight a week later was eerily quiet, almost totally empty and a non-stop service from Bangkok back to Berlin Schönefeld. While I can't say Interflug's Club Class product was an exquisite passenger experience, it was definitely a privilege, a coincidence of fate and history having been able to experience this other German flag carrier so close to its demise. The period around reunification was surely the most turbulent era in Germany's post-war history, and I was lucky I could jump at the chance of experiencing the aviation aspect of it up close and personal. (And I have kept the amenity kit and safety card from this flight to this day.)

Old meets new at Schönefeld Airport   Andreas Spaeth

The end

During the life and times of the GDR, all major enterprise in the country was state-owned, including Interflug. Indeed not only were domestic markets a total monopoly, but even for international trade within the communist bloc, there were rigid agreements between nations covering who built or produced what, and who was going to purchase it (Ukrainian wheat for Moldovan tractors, East German cameras for Cuban sugar cane, et cetera). There was no open market with real competition.

Even before the two Germanys became one, the GDR government began changing course with the winds of change, and created an agency called Treuhand (which translates as Trust Agency), tasked with the privatisation of state-owned companies or, where this was not deemed viable, restructuring or liquidating them. More than 8,500 companies – from steelworks to cucumber factories, and even the famous Babelsberg film studios – fell under the agency's purview, with the livelihoods of more than four million employees affected.

Assessing the value and assets of these state-owned enterprises largely followed the principles of the (Western) free market economy, and in retrospect, were probably applied too strictly in some cases, and carelessly in others.

Of the thousands of companies privatised or restructured after the end of the GDR, only a few became real success stories, such as the optical industry in and around the city of Jena, the IT sector in Dresden, watchmaker Glashütte or the producer of bubbly, Rotkäppchen. Political pressure to restructure and privatise everything quickly led to hasty decisions and more than often, companies were liquidated that could have been saved or restructured with a little bit more time or effort. To be fair, most companies were hugely inefficient by Western standards, massively overstaffed, their equipment old, and their former markets in Eastern Europe more or less gone overnight, all factors which may have worked against them in assessing their value.

Needless to say, although it is hard to make everything right when transferring an entire country from a state-controlled planned economy to free market economy, the numerous liquidations added to the sentiment held by many GDR citizens that they had been annexed or colonised by West Germany, and that by applying rigid Western standards, companies that were working well or producing things of high quality were suddenly regarded as uncompetitive or no longer needed.

Another airline as Interflug's saviour? Even the most hard-boiled optimists had their doubts about Interflug surviving this transition on their own. Finding a strong partner, perhaps another airline, seemed like the best idea, and numerous airlines were targeting Interflug as the target of a takeover bid.

The most obvious choice for a partner was obviously Lufthansa. Long before the major political and economic changes ahead could even be anticipated, several partnerships and agreements between the two airlines had been signed going back to 1984.

An example of this co-operation (and to jumpstart positive relations between both countries), both Interflug and Lufthansa started flights between West Germany and Leipzig during the annual Leipzig trade fair. Lufthansa operated daily flights from Frankfurt, and Interflug served Düsseldorf, Hamburg and Stuttgart. An interline agreement made sure that tickets were accepted mutually, regardless of the operating airline (a practice known as being 'metal-neutral').

When Interflug acquired its three Airbuses a few years later, relations intensified, with maintenance and training contracts signed with Lufthansa. In 1989, Lufthansa's route between Leipzig and Frankfurt became permanent, as did Interflug's services from Leipzig to Düsseldorf, and a new Interflug route between Dresden and Hamburg was added. (None of these flights, however, overflew the Inner German border, so they were all still having to take the detour via a neighbouring country.) In January 1990, both Interflug and Lufthansa announced a couple of joint projects such as a catering unit, and the opening of several new training facilities for flight crews or a maintenance centre at Schönefeld Airport (which even became a reality).

Another very interesting project, in the late summer months of 1990, albeit one which never materialised, was InterCondor. What a catchy name! The quick-witted will have already deduced that this was to be a partnership between veteran German holiday airline Condor (a Lufthansa subsidiary at the time) and Interflug. As Germany was not yet

reunited and Berlin's airports were still under the aegis of the post war political agreement between the Allies and the Soviet Union, West German carriers could still not fly from Schönefeld. Yet, as most of the GDR citizens had quite a bit of catching up to do when it came to travelling to countries beyond the Iron Curtain, a leisure airline based at Schönefeld was deemed a worthwhile project with a lot of potential, and through a partnership with Interflug, Condor wanted to put a towel on the beach as early in the day as possible, in the manner of Germans on holiday everywhere.

Plans called for the initial operation of a single Boeing 757-200 to destinations in Tunisia, Spain, and even long haul to Kenya, Sri Lanka and Thailand. An aircraft was allocated, the first Interflug pilots trained on the type, and a very white livery incorporating the German flag in the tail developed, but alas, despite the optimism, this project never got off the ground. With German reunification on the horizon, it became apparent that Germany would soon regain full sovereignty over its airspace, including all of Berlin's airports. As all German carriers would soon be able to fly from any German airport including those of the soon-to-be-former GDR, the need for a special entity was gone, much to the disappointment of crews that were already trained, and ground staff keen to work for this new carrier.

Despite this disappointment, relations with Condor's parent company Lufthansa kept getting cosier, who remained the most obvious candidate to take over at least part of Interflug. But while both airlines were interested in a deal, their motivations were quite different. Interflug was obviously in the much weaker position, suddenly having to find their way in a completely different environment, and was struggling to survive.

Lufthansa, at the time 51% state-owned, was not in the best shape itself. Its plans for Interflug would have allowed the airline to survive, but it would also have secured Lufthansa an even stronger position in the German domestic market, locked in traffic rights (at least while there were still two Germanys), and brought to heel what could have become a competitor.

In the spring of 1990, Lufthansa announced its intention to acquire a 26 percent stake in Interflug. In an internal survey among Interflug employees, the large majority of them favoured the deal. The Lufthansa supervisory board also unanimously approved it and Lufthansa emphasised its intention to keep Interflug alive as a separate entity, secure jobs and help modernize the airline's ageing fleet. To kick-start the new partnership, Lufthansa agreed to temporarily wet-lease almost the entire fleet of Tu-134s, which operated on new routes between the two newly-unified Germanies under LH flight numbers in full Interflug colours.

But then came a major disappointment: the German cartel office rejected the deal on July 30 as anti-competitive. It argued that Lufthansa was already the dominant entity in the German market, and that this deal would be monopolistic, a decision that both Lufthansa's and Interflug's management could not understand, as to allow Interflug to collapse, would have the same outcome but with the loss of jobs, especially in the former GDR, which if anything needed propping up.

Lufthansa and Interflug did not give up yet, and just a day after the ruling, Lufthansa declared their will to acquire not only 26 but up to 100 percent of the shares of Interflug, establish a new technical base at Schönefeld Airport to be staffed by Interflug employees. It also committed to submitting a sound business plan for the future of Interflug by the middle of September.

While the new offer was being scrutinised by the cartel office, negotiations between the Treuhand and other parties interested in buying a stake in Interflug took place behind closed doors. One of the parties more seriously interested in a takeover of Interflug was British Airways.

At the time, the United Kingdom's flag carrier was in expansion mode, having just taken over British Caledonian, and was looking for other opportunities in the European market. For more than 40 years, the rights to fly from West Berlin, including to other German cities was limited to British, French or US carriers. With German reunification on the horizon, this profitable monopoly was about to end, and as a British carrier, British Airways would no longer be able to fly German domestic routes or from Germany to other countries except the UK.

Full deregulation, which opened up all European routes to all European Union carriers, was only to come into effect in 1993, still a few years down the road. So keen was Britain's aviation industry to enjoy the full benefits of participating in the huge European Union market that British Airways, for a time, seemed willing to acquire a German subsidiary at almost any cost. Other carriers it surveyed were German Wings (no relation to today's Lufthansa subsidiary) and Aero Lloyd. But while no objections were to be expected from the German cartel office, the price British Airways would have had to pay for a meaningful foothold on the German market would have been quite high. Interflug's operation was largely inefficient and overstaffed by Western standards, its debt was quite significant, and its Soviet-built fleet would have been of no use for an airline like British Airways; its only real assets were traffic rights and the ability of any airline using it as a vehicle for a German operation, as British Airways was planning to.

British Airways placed a letter of intent to purchase 49% in Interflug.

For the 1989 Leipzig trade fair, Interflug operated a helicopter shuttle between the city and the airport with this Belgian-registered Agusta-Bell Jet Ranger **Wolfgang Kluge via Bundesarchiv**
Page 154: The sun sets on a perfect Schönefeld ramp scene **Interflug Abteilung Werbung**

Interflug Abteilung Werbung

However, after long negotiations with the Treuhand, British Airways decided against the deal and found what was probably a much less complicated and cheaper solution: a 49% stake in German regional carrier Delta Air, a small airline operating Saab 340s on domestic flights, which later became Deutsche BA and helped British Airways realise their German dream.

When Germany was unified in October 1990, the legal basis for a potential deal with Lufthansa, which was still not completely off the table, changed significantly. It brought Lufthansa into a better negotiation position and Interflug into a worse one. Instead of suggesting a full takeover of Interflug, which was now officially withdrawn, Lufthansa suggested a trustee contract under which Lufthansa would take over Interflug's operations on behalf of the owner and provide the airline's management. After a complete restructuring, Interflug would be evaluated and become a target for takeover by Lufthansa once more. Interflug's management was not in favour of this solution. Its new CEO Andreas Kramer issued a statement claiming that an independent Interflug, operating a fleet consisting of its three extant Airbus A310s, plus eight new Boeing 737s could permanently save around 1,200 jobs even after the necessary cuts; the number of jobs which would be saved should Interflug be fully integrated into Lufthansa would be much lower. Interflug management was not ready to give up the fight yet, rooting for their airline to survive by finding partners other than Lufthansa. But perhaps they overestimated the strength of their position, and the interests of the German political authorities, specifically the Treuhand whose administration they were under, and it was these latter parties who would have the last word.

A few long weeks later, on February 7, 1991, the Treuhand announced that Interflug would be liquidated. A spicy detail in this matter was that the liquidator in charge, Eckart Müller-Heydenreich, who was in favour of keeping Interflug in the air at least until October 1991, fulfil valid charter contracts and streamline the company while seriously looking for a possible new owner for the new airline (or parts of it) was removed from his office on March 7, 1991. His successor in the job, Jobst Wellensiek, a lawyer specialising in company closures, saw things more soberly and a few weeks after joining the new position, he announced on March 26 that flight operations would end just over four weeks later, on April 30, with all domestic flying ceasing even earlier, on April 12.

The sad honour of operating the last ever Interflug revenue service fell to Tu-134A D-AOBC (previously DDR-SCN) on April 30, 1991, the return leg from Vienna back to Berlin-Schönefeld.

Critics say that the decision to let Interflug go was ultimately a political decision that was pushed through without seriously looking at possible survival options. As some branches of Interflug had already been split off from the actual airline (such as the airports and air traffic control, which had all been part of Interflug), 'only' around 2,600 employees were affected by the closure.

Could Interflug have survived on its own? The early 1990s were a difficult time for airlines all over the world, with Iraq's invasion of Kuwait and the US-led war that followed to restore Kuwaiti sovereignty and contain Iraqi dictator Saddam Hussein leading to skyrockering fuel prices and a global downturn in the airline industry.

Airlines in Europe were facing a changing situation with full market liberalisation within the European Union which brought additional opportunities but also an end to local monopolies and duopolies.

It is hard to say how Interflug would have fared. Taken over by a major airline like Lufthansa or British Airways, the airline would probably have shrunk to an operation of around 15 aircraft, most of them 737-sized.

Interflug's role would have been as a niche operator, maybe a charter or low-cost subsidiary for a bigger airline trying to find workarounds to high costs. What is certain is that even a saviour like British Airways or Lufthansa would have made major cuts within the airline, getting rid of much of its staff and all of its Soviet-built fleet. Whether or not the Interflug brand would have survived is a matter of speculation. In the long term, probably not.

In the early 1990s, there was a tendency, now a source of much Ostalgie-tinted regret, to let anything that reminded people of the GDR, including some well-known brands, to simply disappear. Could it have been bad intentions, a lack of sensitivity, or the urge to consign the 45-year division of Germany to the past? Some GDR brands have made a comeback now and have been rediscovered, following a general retro trend.

One of Interflug's assets were traffic rights, which evaporated when the two Germanies became one (which happened much faster than even the most optimistic expectations), making the airline much less attractive as an acquisition target. Airlines considering a takeover bid, simply by waiting, were able to get the market share they wanted without the hassle and expense of having to wrestle Interflug into shape.

Could Interflug have saved by political intervention? Definitely. At least the quite abrupt end it suffered could have been avoided and a company willing to take over at least some parts of the airline probably could have been found. But the political will to keep two state-owned airlines afloat over a longer period, and in the midst of a turbulent period for airlines worldwide, did not exist, which was to the detriment of the weaker of the two, and that was Interflug.

Interflug Abteilung Werbung

Berline: the most successful survivor (at least for a while)

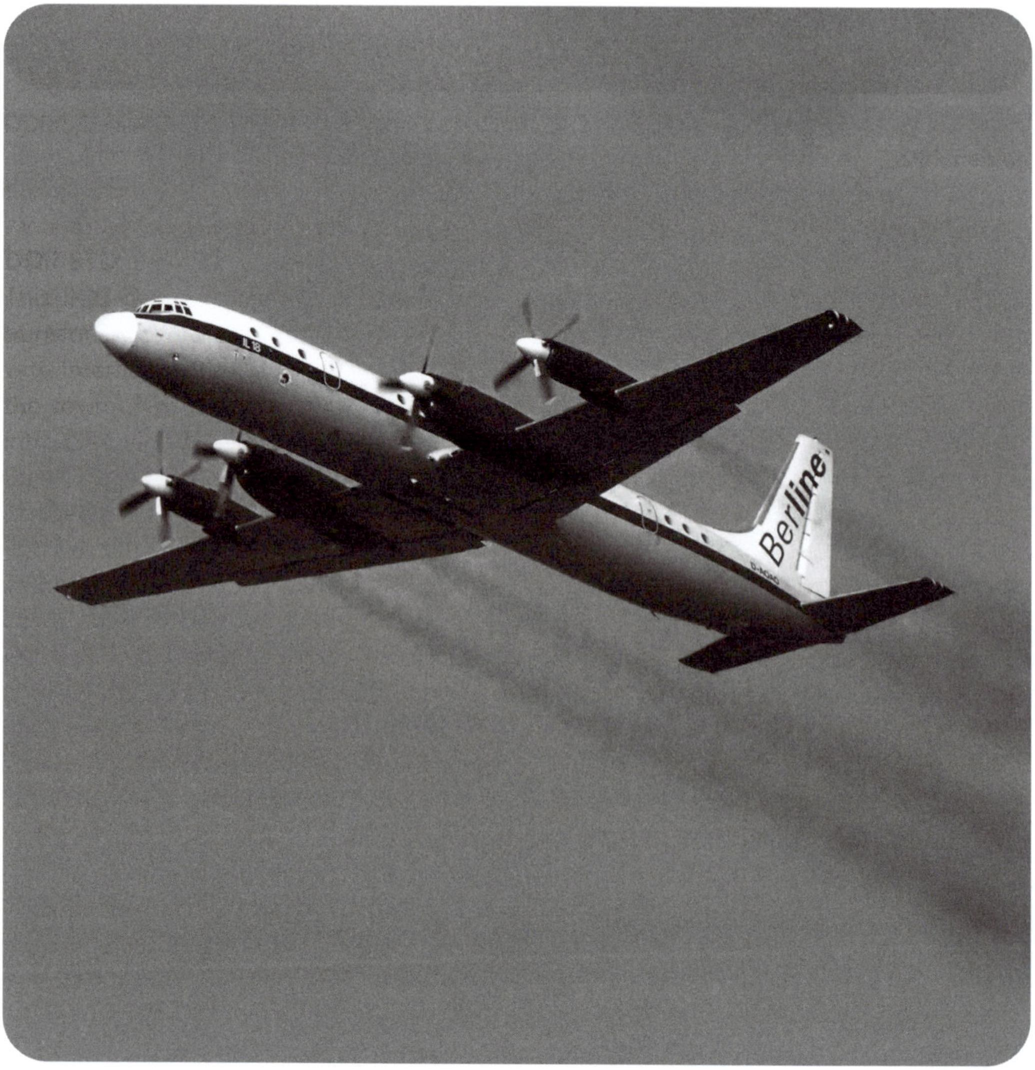

Most Interflug employees, among them around 700 pilots and flight attendants when the airline was liquidated, identified strongly with the carrier. And although many of them found work with other (mostly German) airlines later, the decision by the German Treuhandanstalt, the state agency dealing with the restructuring, privatization or orderly liquidation of former state-owned GDR enterprises, to liquidate the airline came as a quite sudden and major shock to most.

If you ask former Interflug employees about their airline's closure today, more than 25 years later, most still speak of the airline with nostalgia in their voice and you would hear something along the lines: "We were a very fine airline and the closure was absolutely unnecessary." With the prospect of liquidation looming, most of them felt they were up for a good amount of uncertainty and started looking for work opportunities elsewhere long before Interflug was grounded.

When Interflug's management announced that all Il-18s were to be retired by the end of 1990, this decision sparked quite some resistance. For those flying the type, this decision was incomprehensible, as the type was probably the most cost-effective type (even though it was old) in the fleet of Interflug, apart from the three Airbus A310s. They were in good technical condition and were suitable for the most diverse missions (which the type had proven in the last decades). The Il-18 could fly a load of baby chicks to Uzbekistan one day and tourists to the Black Sea on the next. A group of Interflug employees led by flight captain Reinhard Knäblein, most of them flying or otherwise involved with the Il-18, decided to take their fate into their own hands and not become victims of others taking decisions on their behalf.

As so many great things in the world, the idea was born over a few beers to simply start an own airline with the aircraft that they knew inside out, the Il-18, and that would most likely become available for very favourable terms soon, be it before or after the foreseeable end of Interflug, at least as it was. They quite openly questioned and resisted the decision of the Interflug management to retire the type and by announcing they would start their own airline and acquire between three and five Il-18s for it. "IL-18 Air Cargo" was founded and registered with the authorities in early 1990, some time before Interflug stopped flying. When Interflug entered liquidation, four Il-18s were acquired from the liquidator for a symbolic price: D-AOAO (former DDR-STF), D-AOAP (ex DDR-STI), D-AOAS (ex DDR-STM and the only aircraft equipped with a side cargo door) and D-AOAU (former DDR-STO). This quartet was later complemented by a fifth, D-AOAQ (ex DDR-STP), a former calibration aircraft.

What the new airline's management definitely underestimated was the cost to bring the aircraft and documentation fully in line with the requirements of the (West) German civil aviation authority requirements, an investment many times higher than the practically zero acquisition cost and residual value of the five Ilyushins. Well, all obstacles, and that included opposition within Interflug for this initiative, were overcome and an enthusiastic team of pilots, flight attendants and ground staff started flying basically for whoever could find use for these capable aircraft: cargo charters were the new airline's main pillar initially but it soon became obvious that these occasional missions would not be sufficient to keep the carrier afloat. And thus, passenger charters started almost immediately after the airline's launch and the airline's management approached tour operators and charter brokers ffering their service.

The inaugural service took off on November 1, 1991, a charter from Gothenburg in Sweden to Nuremberg and back to the homebase in Schönefeld. To make itself a bit more marketable, the bulky "IL-18 Air Cargo" was changed to a more catchy "Berline", a combination of "Berlin" and "Line" or "Airline" if you will. Interestingly, "Berline" was also the term used for a very popular four-wheeled horse carriage used in and around Berlin in the 17th through the 19th century. Just so you know!

Berline became the first true airline of both Germanys. And at least for some time, it was quite successful. Its fleet of now five Il-18s was kept quite busy, flying cargo missions on behalf of the United Nations, transported chicks and other animals to Russia, carried oil drilling equipment to remote airfields and sunseekers to the Mediterranean, Egypt or the Canary Islands. They were soon painted in a very elegant-looking blue, white and grey colour scheme, replacing the red and white Interflug colours.

Although the Ilyushins were still going strong and capable of flying a lot of very different missions, management soon realized the need for something a bit more modern to satisfy the demands of the average holidaymaker who typically does not appreciate the beautiful inside and outside of an old propeller aircraft. Two Fokker 100s were leased from French airline TAT, F-GIOV and F-GIOX, and

This Il-18 still shows its Interflug heritage along with its new Berline titles, D-AOAO on the unified German register, seen at Bremen in July 1992
Jochen Beeck
Previous page: Smoky takeoff of a Berline Il-18
Luftfahrtarchiv Matthias Winkler

D-AOAO briefly wore this alternative colour scheme, which in the end did not convince
Luftfahrtarchiv Matthias Winkler

Berline's colour scheme shows quite a strong resemblance with the blue and white Deutsche Lufthansa colours of the early days. D-AOAP was the only Il-18 in the fleet to be equipped with a cargo door. **Luftfahrtarchiv Matthias Winkler**

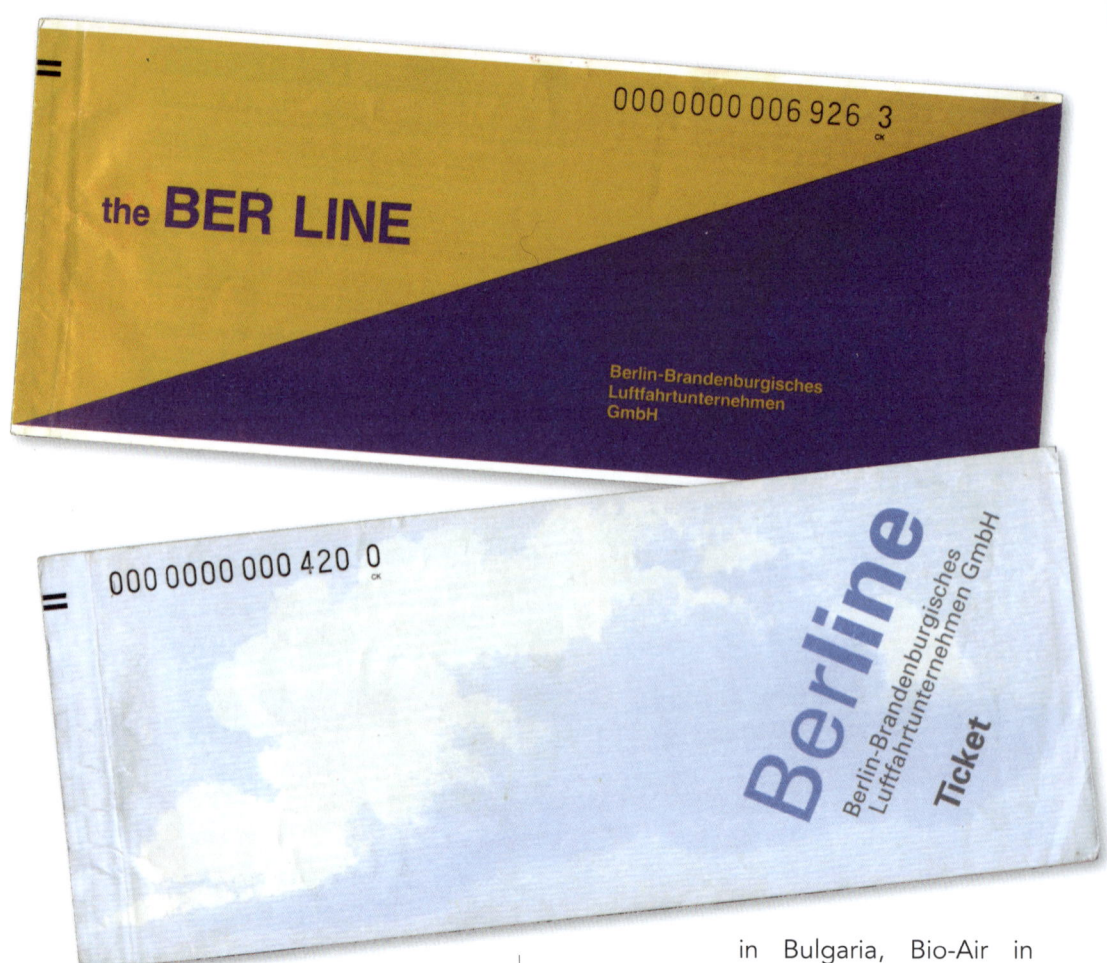

painted in an all silver colour scheme with dark blue Berline colours. Although the two F-100s helped acquiring business that the airline would not have got with the fleet of Il-18s alone, Berline's debt grew and the airline never managed to break even. Regrettably, late 1994, the feisty underdog from the East had to enter bankrupcty proceedings. A relaunch as German European Airlines (two Il-18s were even painted in the new airline's colours) failed when two potential investors turned out to be frauds. The two F-100s were returned, both ending their days with KLM Cityhopper and scrapped in the Netherlands in 2010 and 2011.

Berline's fleet of Il-18s was passed on to all sorts of more or less respectable carriers: D-AOAO flew with Air Zory in Bulgaria, Bio-Air in Bosnia as well as Anikay Air in Kyrgyzstan. It was last registered as EX-405 and photographed at Bishkek Airport, Kyrgyzstan, in deteriorating condition, sporting Anikay Air titles and a very nice blue and red colour scheme, in 2014.

D-AOAP was sold to Russia and registered as RA-75554 after the demise of Berline and sadly ended its flying life in an accident, overrunning the runway at Johannesburg when accelerating for a cargo flight to Bujumbura in 1997. At the time, it was registered to Ramaer Cargo. It was never to fly again, scapped where it stood after being moved from the scene of the smash up.

D-AOAS, the one with the side cargo door, ended up in Cuba as CU-C1515, sporting a beautiful and very Caribbean-inspired colourscheme flying for AeroCaribbean. Unfortunately, it seems to have been out of service for a couple of years now.

D-AOAU also ended up in Cuba with AeroCaribbean as CU-T1532. It suffered an accident during take-off from Holguin Airport on March 6, 2004 and was written off and eventually scrapped. D-AOAQ was sold to Ukraine, first with Air Ukraine and later a small airline called Kryla as UR-74575. It even came back to Germany for a celebrated return, operating sightseeing flights from Schönefeld during an open day there in 2001. It was eventually sold to Angolan operator Alada as D2-FAM. Its current status seems uncertain.

The end of Berline marked the end of a brave initiative of Interflug employees to keep at least part of their airline in the air and keep themselves in gainful employment in a time of economic turmoil. Berline was definitely the most visible successor of Interflug but if - like Interflug itself - it was not to become a long-term success, it still made a splash and was a Berlin favourite in the early years of reunification.

D-AOAO is wearing the logo of ice hockey team BSC Preussen here and seen operating a charter flight on the club's behalf
Luftfahrtarchiv Matthias Winkler

D-AOAO and D-AOAP wearing the colours of German European Airlines, the successor to Berline which never took off
Luftfahrtarchiv Matthias Winkler

Interflug survivors on display

The following aircraft are on display at museums or on private grounds, most of them wearing Interflug or vintage Deutsche Lufthansa colours, as of late 2019. They include Ilyushin Il-14s, Il-18s, Il-62s, Tupolev Tu-134s, and a single surviving Antonov An-24. Except for two aircraft, one in the Netherlands and one in Bulgaria, all are located in Germany and most of them are accessible to the public, some also from inside. Their condition varies from quite sad to excellent but fortunately, all aircraft listed here seem to be in good hands, hopefully keeping the number of future casualties low. (Smaller aircraft and helicopters such as the Antonov An-2, Kamov Ka-26 and Mi-2, which have been operated on agricultural or other non-scheduled services, are not included in the list.)

Antonov An-24
LZ-ANL (ex DM-SBA)
This aircraft is one of two former Interflug aircraft on display outside Germany. The Antonov was delivered to Interflug in 1965 and operated domestic and regional flights for the airline along with five more An-24s until they were all retired in 1976. All sister aircraft were donated to Vietnam, only DM-SBA was passed on to Balkan Bulgarian Airlines, where it was registered LZ-ANL and enjoyed a second career of more than 20 years before it was retired in 1999. Today, it is part of a newly-opened aviation museum at the airport of Bourgas at the Bulgarian Black Sea coast, which was only officially opened in 2017. During the author's visit there in 2017, it was not in very good condition and painted all white. In the meantime, it has been repainted into contemporary Balkan colours and its condition seems at least reasonable.

Museum website:
www.avioburgas.bg

Ilyushin Il-14
DM-SAB
This Ilyushin Il-14 was retired in 1970 and initially stored at the airfield of Barth, close to the Baltic Sea. It was then moved to the town of Caemmerswalde, southwest of Dresden and very close to the Czech border. It is on display there next to the Gaststätte am Flugzeug restaurant, the only of the Ilyushin 14s wearing Interflug colours, and can be visited.

Restaurant website:
www.gaststaetteamflugzeug.de

DM-SAF
Wearing beautiful original Deutsche Lufthansa colours, this Il-14 is another Dresden-built example. It is on display outside the fascinating Hugo Junkers Technikmuseum in Dessau, adjacent to the city's historic airfield. Its last landing

DM-SAB is the only remaining Il-14 wearing Interflug colours. It is on display in the small town of Cämmerswalde, Saxony
Dirk Peisker
Previous page: Il-18 DDR-STE was flown to Borkheide, southwest of Berlin, on 16 November 1989
Sebastian Schmitz

took place in November 1967. Before it got to Dessau, it was in storage in different locations and in increasingly poor condition. Thanks to the tireless work of volunteers, the aircraft is now in very good shape and probably one of the nicest-looking Deutsche Lufthansa / Interflug survivors anywhere.

Museum website:
www.technikmuseum-dessau.de

DM-SAL
The only of the four Il-14s which is not (easily) accessible to the public. It is on display at the Elbe Flugzeugwerke at Dresden Airport, where today Airbuses are converted into freighters or call for heavy maintenance. This is where the Il-14 was built during the early days of Deutsche Lufthansa, in whose colours it is preserved.

Elbe Flugzeugwerke website:
www.elbeflugzeugwerke.com

DM-SAF is wearing full Deutsche Lufthansa colours and on display outside the Technikmuseum "Hugo Junkers" in Dessau
Sebastian Schmitz

DM-ZZB

This is the first prototype of the Il-14 produced in Dresden. Its maiden flight was on October 11, 1955. It was used as a test aircraft and was eventually taken over by Deutsche Lufthansa, later Interflug, and became DM-SAZ. It was retired in 1967 and has since been on display at different location. Today, it is attached to the Barnath car dealership in the small town of Reichenbach, between Zwickau and Plauen, but in increasingly derelict condition.

Car dealer website:
www.barnath.de

Ilyushin Il-18
DDR-STA

Retired from service in 1988, the aircraft deteriorating for a long time at Leipzig/Halle airport. Today, luckily, DDR-STA has been rescued and is on display as a gate guard in front of the airport terminal. It is wearing full Deutsche Lufthansa colours (and the old registration DM-STA) and very easy to photograph.

DDR-STB

Retired in 1987, the aircraft was initially stored in the village of Diepensee. It then had to make room for Berlin's fantastic new airport that is being built there (and at the time of writing, construction is still going on after more than a decade). Today, DDR-STB sits on the rooftop of the Da Capo event hall, oldtimer museum and restaurant in central Leipzig but can unfortunately neither be visited nor photographed really well.

Venue website:
www.michaelis-leipzig.de/de/wir-betreiben/da-capo-oldtimermuseum-und-eventhalle

Il-18 DDR-STA is wearing full Deutsche Lufthansa colours and on display in front of the terminal at Leipzig/Halle Airport
Sebastian Schmitz

DDR-STB has found a new home on the roof of the Da Capo event hall in central Leipzig

Dirk Peisker

DDR-STD

This Il-18 has experienced a remarkable transformation. It was retired from service with Interflug in 1986 and transported to the town of Harbke, close to the former intra-German border. It became the FunnyFly Cafébar, and could also be booked for as a venue for weddings. In 2009, it was taken to the small airport of Teuge in the Netherlands, close to the city of Apeldoorn where it was converted into a luxury hotel suite with all the bells and whistles one would expect. Painted in a grey and white Hotelsuites.nl colour scheme, it features a large bedroom, a jacuzzi, separate shower and sauna as well as three flatscreen TVs. While there is not much Interflug heritage left, the aircraft is in beautiful condition and probably the only Interflug aircraft in which you can comfortably sleep with somebody.

Hotel website: www.vliegtuighotel.nl

DDR-STE

This Il-18 was withdrawn from service with Interflug in November 1989. It was flown to the tiny provisional airfield of Borkheide, southwest of Berlin, where it landed on a short grass runway. It immediately became the star of the Hans-Grade-Museum which commemorates the German aviation pioneer who lived in the village. It is wearing full Interflug colours and can be visited on weekends between May and September by prior arrangement. In autumn 2024, the aircraft was moved to a new location on the airfield site by crane and even though for the 2025 season, the museum seems to be permanently closed, it is probably worth sending them an e-mail when in the area.

Museum website:
www.grade-museum.de

DDR-STG

Happy news from Erfurt in late 2018! This Il-18, which was flown to the airport in late 1988 and since used as a fire trainer, will become a 'flying classroom' – well almost. It was parked on the main apron for years and looked quite sad. However, apprentices from a nearby avionics company and local volunteers have now at least converted the outside into splendid condition. The aircraft has been repainted into full Interflug colours. The aircraft interior will be converted into an interactive learning space where children can learn basics about aviation and environmental issues. It will also become an integral part of airport tours and events. Once fully refurbished, the aircraft will find a home outside the perimeter fence and hopefully be yet another long-term Interflug survivor.

Project website (in German only):
www.spielplatz-der-generationen.de

DDR-STH

Il-18 DDR-STH is the second Interflug passenger aircraft on display at the beautiful Flugausstellung aviation museum in Hermeskeil. Like its old comrade Tu-134 DDR-SCK, it was initially flown to Augsburg upon its retirement. From there, it was taken to Hermeskeil by road a few years later. Painted in full Interflug colours, it is one of the biggest aircraft in the museum's open-air exhibition, open from April to November.

Museum website:
www.flugausstellung.de

DDR-STD has been converted into a very stylish luxury hotel suite at the small airport of Teuge in the Netherlands
Hotelsuites

DDR-STG was recently refurbished and repainted into Interflug colours, looking like fresh out of the factory. It is on display at Erfurt Airport
Manfred Soldan

Ilyushin Il-62
DDR-SEC

This Il-62 was on display in the village of Großmachnow, just south of Schönefeld Airport, for a long time. In 2003, it was moved to Merseburg, where it became part of the Luftfahrt- und Technikmuseum's collection. The museum, however, closed in 2021 and the entire collection´s future seems uncertain. As of 2025, the aircraft remained parked on the airport grounds, wearing full Interflug colours, and seemed in reasonably good shape.

Museum website:
www.luftfahrt-technik-museum.de

DDR-SEF

Flown to Leipzig in 1989, DDR-SEF was parked at the airport for more than two decades. In 2011, it was taken to a new location in central Leipzig and is since in use as a restaurant, freshly-painted in Interflug colours. One happy Interflug survivor! During the summer months, you could sit on the wing and have an ice cream. Right now, the restaurant seems closed and future plans uncertain, but the Il-62 is still in its place

Restaurant website:
www.il62-leipzig.de

DDR-SEG

This is probably the star among all surviving Interflug aircraft. DDR-SEG was flown from Schönefeld to the small airfield of Stölln (see separate chapter in this book) and spectacularly landed there on a grass runway. It has since been the key component of the Otto-Lilienthal-Museum whose volunteers take loving care of the aircraft, christened Lady Agnes after aviation pioneer Lilienthal's wife.

Museum website:
www.otto-lilienthal.de

Tupolev Tu-134
DDR-SCB

Retired in November 1985 after a hard landing in Schönefeld, DDR-SCB was initially moved to the city of Oschersleben and on display there for several years. Unfortunately, it got quite neglected and was only saved in 2004, when it was moved to a new location at Magdeburg Airport. It was refurbished and is today on display next to the airport restaurant in full Interflug colours.

Magdeburg Airport website:
www.edbm.de

Cabin interior of Tu-134 DDR-SCZ, on display at Merseburg Airport
Marius Höpner
Previous page: DDR-SCL was purchased by Hydro Systems and is today on display at the company headquarters in Biberach
Hydro

Tu-134 DDR-SCK is on display in the beautiful Flugausstellung close to the town of Hermeskeil together with Il-18 DDR-STH Sebastian Schmitz

DDR-SCH

After its retirement in December 1983, DDR-SCH was used as a training aircraft for mechanics at Schönefeld Airport. In 1992, it was moved to the Luftfahrtmuseum in Finowfurt, next to the airport of Eberswalde-Finow, northeast of Berlin. It was in full Interflug colours until it was partially painted in LOT Polish Airlines colours for a movie shoot. Today, it is still wearing that interesting hybrid colours.

Museum website is: www.luftfahrtmuseum-finowfurt.de

DDR-SCK

One of two former Interflug Tu-134s on display in western Germany is DDR-SCK. Put out of service in September 1990, it was flown to the airport in Augsburg together with Il-18 DDR-STH to join a museum there. A few years later, in 1994, both aircraft were transported to the Flugausstellung Hermeskeil, a very comprehensive aviation museum close to the town of the same name, north of Saarbrücken. It is in very good condition and wearing full Interflug colours.

Museum website: www.flugausstellung.de

DDR-SCL

DDR-SCL was retired in early 1990 and purchased by Hydro Systems, a company specialising in the production of ground support equipment and other supplies for the aviation industry. Its last flight went from Berlin to the former Canadian Forces Base Lahr, via a stop in Stuttgart. Within three days the aircraft was dismantled into transportable parts in Lahr and taken to the Hydro headquarters in the town of Biberach on low-loaders where it was re-assembled. A bit sad for purists, the aircraft has been painted into the company's own blue and white colours but at least it is receiving very good attention.

Hydro website: www.hydro.aero

DDR-SCZ

The last of the remaining Interflug Tu-134s on display was retired from service with the airline in March 1986. Initially on display in Bernsdorf, it is now part of the collection of the Luftfahrt-und-Technikmuseum Merseburg together with former Interflug Il-62 DDR-SEC. As the museum closed recently, both aircraft´s future seems bleak. As of 2025, it remains parked outside the museum and definitely in need of a proper cleanup and new paintjob, as the long time in the open air is taking its toll.

Museum website: www.luftfahrt-technik-museum.de

IF
A village with an Ilyushin

Not many towns can boast what the tiny village of Stölln, around an hour's drive northwest of Berlin can: its own Ilyushin Il-62. Registered DDR-SEG and painted in full Interflug colours, this bird probably has the most fascinating story of any Interflug survivor, and its last landing, which took place on October 23, 1989, is also part of another very interesting story, the life of one of Germany's most famous pilots, Heinz-Dieter Kallbach.

Just outside the village of Stölln, at the foot of the Gollenberg hill, there is still an active airfield today, which even has an ICAO code, EDOR. The hill nearby is where German aviation pioneer Otto Lilienthal undertook most of his revolutionary glider flights in the late 19th century. Most of them were successful, except for the last one, in which Lilienthal and his glider stalled and crashed from around 15 metres (50 feet) up. He broke his neck and died the next day.

The airfield is operated by the Otto Lilienthal aviation sports club and boasts a single grass runway, 08/26, measuring 900 x 40 metres (2,953 x 131 feet), which is apparently enough to accomodate an occasional Il-62 landing. There are also two towing sections for winch launches south of the runway, and two additional landing areas for gliders between the towing sections, one at each end of the airfield. Other than the occasional glider or light aircraft (anything up to an An-2), there is very little going on here and the busiest days are summer weekends. The main attraction for visitors is the parked Ilyushin and the museum and visitor centre nearby.

And this is how the Il-62 got here. In spring 1988, Stölln's industrious mayor, Sybille Heling, came up with the idea to establish a permanent monument preserving the legacy of Otto Lilienthal and thought of an aircraft that could be parked here. Interflug's CEO at the time, Klaus Henkes, warmed to the idea and decided that either an Il-18 or Il-62 could be donated to the town and put on display, accessible to visitors in this historic location. Aircraft of both types were about to be retired from service with the airline in the near future but financing remained unclear (the small municipality was to be charged for the scrap value of the aircraft, the costs of the flight and the necessary preparation of the landing site).

The mayor was torn: while she did not want to reject this very attractive donation, she also could not afford it, as the costs exceeded the budget of the little town. On August 8, 1988, she received a redemptive phone call from Interflug HQ that changed everything: the airline would not charge any scrap value costs nor charge the village for the costs of the actual flight. All that Stölln was responsible for was to prepare the landing strip. Amazing news! And the

Locals enjoying their coffee in front of the museum café - many of them probably former Interflug staff
Previous page:
Reigning over the village, Il-62 DDR-SEG
Sebastian Schmitz

aircraft type was also chosen: as an Il-18 was going to be donated to the museum at Borkheide, Stölln was going to get an Il-62. Which made things even more challenging.

The mayor and other influential people from the area decided to go ahead with this amazing and challenging project – and had the full support of the Ministry of Transport. One of the key figures inside Interflug (and the pilot who would actually be flying this mission) was Heinz-Dieter Kallbach, former fleet captain of Interflug's Il-62 fleet and still an active Il-62 captain at the time. He also held a key position in the Ministry of Transport.

Kallbach became a pilot by coincidence. As a child, he did not have to attend physical education lessons because of three brain concussions he suffered previously. At that time, this ruled out career as a pilot. After the war, when the National People's Army was founded, volunteers were urgently needed. While it seemed clear that he would not become a pilot, upon signing up for service with the army, Kallbach enrolled to become an aviation mechanic, albeit at that time he was only 16, too young actually to start the course. The day came for the entrance exam, and it turned out that everyone else in the room was a pilot candidate. So without ever imagining a chance to become a pilot himself, Kallbach passed the exams and medical tests which were actually for future pilots. He kept quiet about his prior medical condition and was accepted by the flying school at Bautzen in 1957. Suddenly he was going to become a pilot after all.

When the instructor talked to him for the first time and found out that Kallbach had never seen an aircraft before (some of his colleagues had flown glider planes or similar), it was decided that flying a Yakovlev Yak-11 and becoming a fighter pilot would be too much for him. If he wanted to fly, it would be as a transport pilot on the Antonov An-2, which was fine with him, as he had never expected to become a pilot at all.

During his army years, Kallbach met a girl who had relatives in the West and a relationship with her ruled out a military career. But once more, there was a Plan B: Deutsche Lufthansa was just being built up and was desperately looking for pilots. His commander talked to him and asked whether he could imagine flying for the airline instead of the military. Of course! He was the youngest pilot in the army at 18 and a few years later, the youngest captain flying the Ilyushin Il-14 at 24. He later converted to the much bigger Il-18, where he started out as a co-pilot again, and also flew the Antonov An-24 for a while, an interesting experience as he recalls, but not the same type of flying as on the Il-18.

After pursuing a university degree to become an engineer, Kallbach returned to the flying job and resumed flying his beloved Il-18, a type he became an instructor on. Flying the Il-18 for Interflug took him to the most obscure corners of the world. As well as many European cities, he remembers flying to Asia and Africa. In a mix of scheduled and solidarity flights, Dar es Salaam, Cairo, Addis Ababa, Maputo, Conakry, Lagos, and Luanda all appear in his logbook.

On one flight from Mozambique back to the GDR, an intermediate stop was scheduled in N'Djamena, the capital city of Chad. The landing was at night, which was unusual for that airport. The flight was met by a very sleepy ramp agent who, after placing the chocks, ended up in one of the still running engines, got severely injured and died soon later. Fortunately, most of his other memories flying the Il-18 are much happier and Kallbach says that it was on the 18 that he really perfected his flying skills.

Following the introduction of the Il-62, he converted to that type and flew it for 12 years. The Il-62 is completely different to the Il-18. It is much faster, the early non-M birds did not have hydraulic power for the control surfaces, so being a pilot was relatively hard physical work. The approach speed was very high at 340 km/h, which made crosswind landings challenging.

Just like the Il-18, Kallbach only has good things to say about the Il-62. It was a joy to fly, in 12 years on the type, he never suffered an engine failure (which he did on all the other types he flew). Being a training captain and eventually the chief pilot for the Il-62 from 1983, Kallbach not only performed test flights after maintenance

A fitting retirement for a hardworking Soviet jet   Sebastian Schmitz

DDR-SEG's interior is fitted out with a wide range of artifacts from Interflug's illustrious past
Sebastian Schmitz

but also operated inaugural flights on new routes or special flights like a charter to Calgary, carrying the GDR delegation to the Winter Olympics in 1988. Destinations he remembers are Beijing, Singapore, Tokyo, Bangkok, Karachi, Khabarovsk (a stop on the way to Tokyo), of course Moscow and Saint Petersburg, many African ports, Cuba (with a stop in Gander), Nicaragua, Rio de Janeiro, and Montevideo in South America.

The inaugural flight to Montevideo was another very eventful flight for Kallbach and the crew. With a stop in Dakar en route, a crew change was supposed to take place. One crew was supposed to be positioned out on KLM a few days in advance, to then take over and fly on to Montevideo. Unfortunately, the positioning crew, upon arrival in Dakar, did not have Senegalese visas in their passports (as the GDR's understanding was that they were not necessary, as airline crews are exempt in most countries). What was supposed to be a nice three-day layover in sunny Senegal became three days in jail for the crew. They were only released once the Interflug aircraft landed from Berlin and they were released to operate the second leg to Montevideo.

While East and West Germany relations gradually transitioned from hostile to more pragmatic over the years, diplomatic interference was not uncommon. Once, during the stop in Gander Newfoundland, the aircraft was searched for weapons by the Canadians, as the West German secret service were sure they had knowledge of dubious boxes being loaded onto the plane from a helicopter. Nothing was found. Another time, in Madagascar, the aircraft was temporarily confiscated, just as the crew were about to start engines, another West German initiative apparently. Usually, however, relations between the two Germanies, at least as far as aviation was concerned, were not great, but not very tense either.

Under the supervision of Kallbach, Interflug was the first airline to operate the Il-62 with a four cockpit crew instead of the usual five. Two pilots, a flight engineer and a navigator was all, dispensing with the role of a radio operator. Contact with air traffic control was conducted by the pilots when close to the airport, and by the navigator during cruise.

But let us return to the spectacular landing of Il-62 DDR-SEG in Stölln. When Kallbach first heard of the plan to land an Il-62 on 900 meters of grass. he thought the idea was totally crazy. At the same time, he was intrigued by the idea, and wanted to find a solution to what seemed to be a reckless mission. He started calculating...

The empty weight of the Il-62 was 83 tons. How much lighter could the aircraft be made? Could the aircraft be stopped on this sensationally short grass runway? His calculations, with all the various factors such as a row of trees close to the arrival end of the runway in mind, brought him to a maximum weight of 75 tons. The Il-62 would have to be made eight tons lighter. Not an easy task, but seemed doable. Interflug management assured him of their full support and technicians started their calculations. Everybody was keen to make this work somehow. All seats were taken out, the heavy tail wheel and the auxiliary power unit in the rear removed. All this made the aircraft a lot lighter in the back. Which was good, because under normal circumstances, water ballast was carried in the front for trim reasons, which was now no longer necessary. The last ton of weight reduction that was needed was 'calculated away', as Kallbach puts it.

Another way for Kallbach to save weight and minimise the risk for human lives was to operate with minimum crew. He contacted Ilyushin for a special permit to fly the Il-62 with only the captain and a flight engineer, which was rejected.

Preparations on the ground also started immediately once this project was given the green light: a few hectares of forest were cleared, mostly to give the pilots better views of the landing site, sand was piled up, and the touchdown zone was paved. The costs of operation amounted to around 100,000 marks, still a lot of money for a small town. And even with a significant amount of preparations on the ground, a short grass runway remains a short grass runway and landing an Il-62 here remained, to put it mildly, a challenging mission. After a year of intensive preparations and calculations, the big day came on October 23, 1989. The autumn day dawned with good and sunny conditions, a positive omen for the mission at hand. The crowd assembled to welcome the flight was so large, it seemed like the entire village (or more) was out to witness this spectacular landing.

Even with all reserves in mind, it was absolutely essential to nail the touchdown point, on top of a small hill, accurately. After the short flight from Schönefeld airport, Kallbach and his crew performed two very low overflights.

During the final approach, the two inner engines were shut down and reverse thrust on the two outer engines was selected at an altitude of 50 metres (164 feet), allowing time for the engines to wind down to flight idle power, and then spool up to full reverse thrust at the moment of touchdown, a sequence that takes around seven or eight seconds, precious time that would have been lost on the ground. The spoilers were

The dramatic arrival of DDR-SEG captured in mid-bounce

extended immediately after touchdown, and the nose was held high in the air by Kallbach for as long as possible to create aerodynamic drag by presenting the belly of the fuselage as a huge airbrake. At around 140 km/h ground speed, the nose came down and dug a lane around 25 cm deep into the ground, as did the main gear.

Kallbach's calculation foresaw a landing distance of 868 meters (2,848 feet). In the event, only 800 meters (2,625 feet) was used. The landing had been noisy and dramatic, with the enormous Il-62 coming to a halt in an enormous cloud of dust. The three pilots did not have a clue at first where they were or even whether the landing had been a success. Also, they had expected the two running engines to get completely destroyed by the dust. Which was not the case. Once the dust had settled, with two functioning engines, they decided to taxi the aircraft to its final resting place under its own power. The two inner engines were pushed up and under the eyes of an amazed crowd, the aircraft taxied up the little hill to where it stands today. What a glorious landing!

Today, the Ilyushin, christened *Lady Agnes* after Lilienthal's wife, houses a very nice museum, and is definitely a worthy monument for Otto Lilienthal. It is also used for wedding ceremonies. Members of the active Otto-Lilienthal-Verein club undertake every effort to keep the aircraft in perfect condition both inside and out. Donations are gratefully received! Museum exhibits include service items such as trolleys and other equipment, Interflug uniforms, aircraft models, a large world map with Interflug's destinations, photographs, and other items and documents that were donated by Interflug passengers or former employees over the years.

After the end of his career with Interflug, where he flew the Airbus A310 in the end, Heinz-Dieter Kallbach joined private German carrier Germania and flew the Boeing 737 there. He got famous once more when on one of his flights an attempted hijacking was resisted, although he got injured. Flying for a private airline (which later went bankrupt) was completely different to his life with Interflug, a time he often misses when looking back. Being part of Interflug felt like being member of a big family.